The GLASGOW AND WEST COAST Cook Book

A celebration of the amazing food & drink on our doorstep.
Featuring over 45 stunning recipes.

The Glasgow Cook Book

©2018 Meze Publishing Ltd. All rights reserved.

First edition printed in 2018 in the UK.

ISBN: 978-1-910863-43-5

***Thank you to: Peter McKenna and Ivan Stein,
The Gannet, Ryan James, Two Fat Ladies***

Compiled by: Jo Mallinder

Written by: Paul Trainer

*Photography by: Clair Irwin
(www.clairirwinphotography.com)*

Edited by: Phil Turner, Katie Fisher

Designed by: Matt Crowder, Paul Cocker

*Contributors: Sarah Koriba, David Wilson,
Izzy Randall, Amy Clarke, Sam Hancock,
Sally Zaki*

Cover art: Luke Prest (www.lukeprest.com)

Printed by: Bell and Bain Ltd, Glasgow

Published by Meze Publishing Limited
Unit 1b, 2 Kelham Square
Kelham Riverside
Sheffield S3 8SD
Web: www.mezepublishing.co.uk
Telephone: 0114 275 7709
Email: info@mezepublishing.co.uk

FOREWORD

Ivan Stein and Peter McKenna, chef-owners at The Gannet,
invite you to enjoy a snapshot of Glasgow cooking.

We both moved to Glasgow and chose to open our restaurant on Argyle Street. We wanted to add something different to the food scene. We connected with the city on a personal level and our business has grown from there.

Looking around the city and the west of Scotland, we're inspired by the amazing food producers that surround us. Transforming their ingredients – venison, langoustines, beef, vegetables, foraged herbs – into outstanding dishes is our passion.

Restaurants need to be accessible and inclusive. This book is a wonderful way to discover where our food comes from, how it is prepared, and how that reflects the place that we live in.

Take this cook book as inspiration and go look for the best produce you can find, get to know your local restaurants a bit better and try out the recipes at home.

When you put a bit of work into a good meal to share with family or friends, you can taste the difference. Cooking should be a joy, part of everyone's daily life. Learn different techniques and try out new types of cuisine. Each season brings its own fantastic selection of flavours to experiment with.

We both feel part of a very interesting and exciting moment for the restaurant scene in Glasgow. It's all happening right here and this cook book is a great roadmap to the best recipes in the city.

Peter McKenna and Ivan Stein
The Gannet

A taste of
GLASGOW

Restaurateur Ryan James of Two Fat Ladies at The Buttery invites you to connect with local food stories.

I'm delighted to see the collection of recipes in The Glasgow and West Coast Cook Book, which demonstrates what an exciting time it is for food in the city. We're bucking against the trend with independents continuing to do well. There's smaller restaurants that have come through the ranks at food festivals and are now finding their place in local neighbourhoods.

We are part of the communnity here in Anderston and Finnieston with Two Fat Ladies at The Buttery and we've seen a lot of young creatives move into the area. Across the city you can look at areas like Shawlands, Dennistoun, Great Western Road, Strathbungo, Battlefield and you see a burgeoning café scene. There's a real buzz about restaurants that are attracting people to different areas of the city and giving a sense of identity to the place.

Reading through the food stories and recipes in this book, you'll see Glasgow's food culture is as strong as it has ever been. I hope that people will take up the invitation to try all these recipes, find the best local ingredients and have some fun in the kitchen.

We all want Glasgow to flourish and to be a desirable area for independent businesses to open. We try to look out for each other. The mavericks tend to stick together. If you like that attitude, then go out and visit your favourite local restaurant.

The Glasgow and West Coast Cook Book also shows what a very eclectic, multicultural scene we have in the city, that's linked in with the local producers. That's the key.

Glasgow as a food city has always had a good restaurant scene, but there's a sense of things coming together at the moment and books like this help join the dots for people.

We're attracting more visitors to Glasgow all the time and they should know they can expect some exceptional food while they are here. You can join in when you try one of these recipes at home, or go out for dinner to keep the 2,000 or so restaurants in Glasgow going.

Ryan James – Two Fat Ladies

People make
GLASGOW

Officially the World's Friendliest City, you're guaranteed a warm welcome in Glasgow, but there is so much more on offer in this vibrant, colourful and exciting destination.

If you are lucky enough to call it home, Glasgow provides constant reminders of its distinctive culture, lively spirit and strength of character.

Packed with award-winning places to eat, you can easily spend your entire time in the city dining in top class restaurants. Glasgow's story is one of constant reinvention and the way it approaches Scottish cuisine is no exception.

Creative cooking and a vibrant social scene combine for an outstanding dining experience. The Merchant City and the West End have long established restaurants that are part of the fabric of Glasgow hospitality. Then there are burgeoning food scenes in areas like Finnieston, Shawlands and Dennistoun, attracting attention for innovative cooking.

Pop-up restaurants abound and street food markets have become a showcase for emerging culinary talent. Meanwhile, an ever-increasing menagarie of cooking styles and international influences are contributing to the local mix. Beyond the city, a short trip takes you to some glorious countryside where they serve up the best of Scottish produce.

The Glasgow and West Coast Cook Book brings you closer to the people and recipes behind local success. Bring a flavour of the city to your own kitchen, then get to know your new favourite restaurant and the community that surrounds it.

Beyond the burgeoning food scene, there are plenty of other reasons to visit Glasgow. There is an amazing selection of art galleries and museums, including the stunning Kelvingrove Art Gallery and Museum, The Gallery of Modern Art and the Riverside Museum. The city's civic art and museum collection is one of the finest in Europe, cementing the city's reputation as Scotland's cultural powerhouse.

Glasgow is a UNESCO City of Music with legendary venues to discover, from small, intimate spaces right through to the 13,000 seater SSE Hydro Arena. The city stages an impressive 130 music events in a typical week, ranging from pop and rock to Celtic and opera.

Even if you feel like you know the Glasgow story, there's still more to discover for yourself. As you walk around and explore the city, remember to look up; stunning architecture is everywhere, from the neo gothic majesty of Glasgow Cathedral and the Victorian splendour of the City Chambers in George Square, right through to the ultra-modern Glasgow Science Centre.

You'll also encounter impactful, creative and downright quirky art in the streets you walk along thanks to the city's mural trail. Dozens of murals are located throughout the city centre, adding vibrant splashes of colour.

The inspirational work of Glasgow-born architect, designer and artist Charles Rennie Mackintosh, a pioneer of Art Nouveau, is the pride of the city and a not-to-be-missed experience. Discover the unique magic of his work at attractions such as House for an Art Lover, Scotland Street School and the wonderfully restored Tea Rooms at Mackintosh at the Willow.

You can bag a bargain too; boasting the best shopping in the UK outside London, Glasgow has an enormous variety on offer, from high street favourites to vintage boutiques and craft markets. The city's Style Mile is the perfect place to head for the ultimate retail experience.

Explore the distinct neighbourhoods of Glasgow, each with their own personality, vibe and hidden gems as well as local foodie experiences. The city is easy to get around, so whether you live here, or are visiting, take time to go beyond the familiar and you'll find a wealth of memorable people and places.

For more information and to plan your time in the city visit peoplemakeglasgow.com

Elixir OF LIFE

Glasgow Taxis are the largest supplier of licensed taxis in the city.
George McIntosh has over 30 years experience as a taxi driver and shares his
thoughts on a journey through the Merchant City.

George sees the changes. He can track the evolution of the Glasgow night-time economy as he ferries folk around the streets of the city. "What's actually happening now, is the scene is being led by the restaurants and folk going out to eat. I navigate between food places more than bars now when I'm working in the city centre. You get to hear about the places that are doing well. Some folk will describe their entire meal to you," he says, laughing.

"For me, it's interesting to see how many people are out during the week and going to restaurants more. It's not just at the weekend. Folk will give me recommendations for new places to try all the time. You see them dressed up for a night and they are excited about about what they are going to have to eat, you can tell when they get into the cab. Often we'll end up having a great conversation about Glasgow food.

"It's a great thing for the city, and it makes for a pleasant journey. When customers jump in the cab after they've had a good feed, they are at their happiest."

Glasgow Taxis' fleet ensures that diners find the right restaurant and make it to their reservation in time. In the evenings, NiteZone taxi ranks have additional lighting and

Homesafe Marshals manage the queue, making sure people get home safely and quickly. They operate Friday and Saturday nights between 11pm and 4am. "It means you can relax when it comes time to make your way up the road," George says.

Working nightshifts, George was involved with starting a special Glasgow Taxis tradition. He has a recipe of his own to share. "We started making a big bowl of soup for after we'd be finished up, maybe 3am on a Friday, we'd serve it to the drivers and the stewards. It's always the same soup, has been for about 20 years.

"We made it as cheap and as tasty as possible. You'd be feeding maybe ten folk...

"Here's what you do. One bag of frozen leeks. A third of a block of butter. Put that in a pot. Heat it up until the leeks are cooked. Add half a dozen stock cubes. Blitz that with a hand blitzer. Then you add your totties. Mix it all up and keep cooking it. Add water. Boil that up. Double cream. Salt and pepper. We call it the Glasgow Taxis Elixir of Life. We've not met anybody that doesn't like it."

To book a Glasgow Taxi call 0141 429 7070 or use their free app, available on iPhone and Android.

CONTENTS

Editorial

Foreword	4
A taste of Glasgow	6
People make Glasgow	8
Elixir of life	12
Food for a Glasgowist	18
The directory	184

Chef recipes

Brian Maule at Chardon d'Or
Confit lamb fillet with dauphinoise potatoes, spinach
and shiitake mushroom — 21

The Ubiquitous Chip
Lamb neck, aubergine pureé, artichoke, roast tomato — 23

Madha Indian
Nalli gosht — 25

Bilson Eleven
Loch Etive trout sashimi with verdita sauce — 27

Café Gandolfi
Black pudding with mushrooms and pancakes — 29

A'Challtainn
This is the plaice — 30
Plaice and clams with grapefruit emulsion — 33

Alla Locanta
The Mediterranean lifestyle — 34
Sultan kebabs — 37

Da Luciano
Gnocchi da Luciano — 39

Sannino Pizzeria
Linguine frutti di mare — 41

Baffo Pizza & Birra
Kelvingrove's taste of Italy — 42
Tiramisu: a family recipe — 45

Basta
Pizza party — 46
Cullen skink pizza — 49

Battlefield Rest
Southside special — 50
Smoked haddock risotto with Stornoway
black pudding and crispy egg — 53

Billington's of Lenzie
Deli life in Lenzie — 54
Baked chicken with Italian taleggio cheese and pesto — 57

Catch
Catch of the day — 58
Lobster roll — 61

é Pasta e Basta
What a guy — 62
Squid ink tagliolini with king scallops and monkfish — 65
Hand-cut pappardelle with beef fillet
and cherry tomatoes — 67

The Fish People Café
Power to the people — 68
Tandoori sea bass — 71

Fruin Farm
Country life — 72
Ginger braised Puddledub pig's cheeks — 75

Gamba
Fresh is best — 76
Foup with Portland crab meat, stem ginger and
coriander — 79

The Gannet
A Finnieston feast — 80
Sweet cicely cured herring — 83

Gather by Zique
From farm to plate — 84
Roast lamb rack with celeriac caponata — 87

Glasgow Distillery – Makar Gin
Making their makar 90
Makar gin cocktails 93
Halloumi
Get yourself to the Greek 94
Spanakopita 97
Bibimbap
Korean fried chicken 99
Pickled Ginger
Volcano roll 101
Rioja
Suckling pig with Iberian chorizo and ham 103
La Bonne Auberge
The French connection 104
Confit duck, creamed cabbage, smoked bacon,
pine nuts and potato rosti 107
Leiper's Attic
Top of their game 108
Pheasant breast, apple and cider jus, shallot and kale 111
Lodge on Loch Lomond
Fine dining on the loch 112
Venison 115
Lychee Oriental
Eastern promise 116
Char siu roast pork 119
Mussel Inn
Hooked on Hope Street 120
Mini seafood platter 123
Peppered mackerel pâté 125
Nanika
Small room big flavours 126
Wuhan sesame noodles 129
The Oystercatcher
Loch Fyne dining 130
Whole chilli crab 133
Partick Duck Club
Everything it's quacked up to be 134
Duck leg, crispy duck egg, duck fat fries, spiced and
smoked pineapple chutney 138
Piece
Passion and guts 139
The jerkoff 141

RUSK & RUSK
Food with style 142
Hutchesons City Grill
Whole lemon sole with buerre blanc,
lemon and parsley 145
The 158 Club Lounge
Parma violet 147
The Butchershop Bar and Grill
Soft shell crab with celeriac miso remoulade 149
So L.A.
Chickpea panisse, cauliflower and almond purée,
Puy lentil and squash salad 151
The Spanish Butcher
Iberica de bellotta with manchego truffle fries
and mojo verde sauce 153
Sloans
A twist on the classic 154
Legendary macaroni cheese 157
Spitfire Espresso
Smell the coffee 158
Super simple spitfire brownies 161
Sugar Boat
Life is sweet 162
Bouillabaisse 165
Tantrum Doughnuts
Dough idea 166
Old-fashioned buttermilk doughnuts 169
Two Fat Ladies
Classic cooking 170
West coast scallops, golden raisin and saffron purée,
spiced cauliflower fritters 173
Wild Fig
Wild about cooking 174
Baked scottish hake, potato and sausage fabada 177
The Winged Ox
Calton calling 178
Shepherd's pie, cauliflower, crispy kale
and roasted onions 181

Food for a
GLASGOWIST

A sprawling series of conversations with chefs and visits to restaurants led to this book: a fully-formed testament to local food that's worth celebrating. Food writer Paul Trainer introduces your new kitchen inspiration.

This book started as a scribble on a piece of paper during a meal in Café Gandolfi. I decided I wanted to write a book about Glasgow restaurants even before I began to chronicle the best food places in the city at Glasgowist.com. It remained the kernel of an idea until I came across Meze Publishing's regional cook book series, which had become a success across the country. I knew that Glasgow had recipes and stories that deserved to be shared. The team at Meze agreed.

Like all your favourite recipes, The Glasgow and West Coast Cook Book is greater than the sum of its parts. For a start, it is twice the size we thought it would be, uniting the finest chefs in the west of Scotland. The book became more than a collection of restaurant dishes to try at home. It's a portrait of where we live right now, through the food that we eat, the people that make it and the neighbourhoods that they enliven.

When you stay in a place long enough, it is easy to progressively tune out the background noise on familiar streets. If you live here, take this book as an invitation to look up, rediscover the city and explore the communities beyond.

The Glasgow and West Coast Cook Book has been an epic, joyous collaboration. Make it part of your home. Take it to your kitchen. Get cooking. Visit the varied independents you will meet on these pages.

We'll start with three meditations on lamb from local favourites, a quick and impressive fish recipe from a rising star in Dennistoun and how to make the dish I was eating when I first had the idea that became this book. After that, it's a cavalcade of flavours and local characters.

This book wouldn't have been possible without the shining talent and spirit of the Glasgow and West Coast food scene, the exceptional photographs of Clair Irwin, alongside the relentless enthusiasm and enduring patience of Meze Publishing.

For my own introduction to Glasgow food, I would like to thank my family.

While tastes change and culinary trends ebb and flow, one piece of local advice from Sir Billy Connolly still rings true:

"Go to Glasgow at least once in your life and have a roll and square sliced sausage and a cup of tea. When you feel the tea coursing over your spice-singed tongue, you'll know what I mean when I say: It's good to be alive."

Paul Trainer writes at Glasgowist.com

Brian Maule at Chardon d'Or

CONFIT LAMB FILLET WITH DAUPHINOISE POTATOES, SPINACH AND SHIITAKE MUSHROOM

Whenever Glasgow's best chefs are mentioned, Brian Maule is invariably near the top of the list. His restaurant on West Regent Street has been showered with awards and continues to provide the highest standard of fine dining in the city. This is a dish that can be prepared in advance of a dinner party for an outstandingly tasty meal.

Preparation time: 30 minutes | Cooking time: 2 hours | Serves: 4

Ingredients

4 Scotch lamb neck fillets

150g rock salt

1 litre duck fat

3 large Rooster potatoes

600ml double cream

Salt and pepper, to taste

100g shiitake mushrooms

Drizzle of olive oil

600g fresh spinach

100g butter

100g fresh rosemary

Method

For the lamb

Trim the excess sinew off the fillets. Cut into small, even pieces and coat both sides in rock salt. Leave for 1 hour then remove the salt. Melt the duck fat and place the lamb pieces in, cover with a cartouche and oven cook slowly at about 150°c. When cooked, remove from the fat, place on a tray and cover with cling film until needed.

For the dauphinoise

Peel and slice the potatoes thinly then mix them gently with 500ml of the double cream and season with salt. Place in a roasting dish, cover with tin foil and bake in the oven for 2 hours on a low heat. Remove the tray from the oven every 20 minutes and press down the mix with another tray, to ensure that when it's time to cut the dauphinoise for presentation it doesn't fall apart. Leave to cool and then cut into neat rings before serving.

For the mushrooms and spinach

Clean and wash the shiitake mushrooms. Fry lightly in a pan with olive oil (about 3 minutes or until tender) then drain off the excess liquid. Pick and wash the spinach and drop into boiling salted water to cook for 30 seconds. Remove and place straight into iced salted water; this stops the spinach cooking further and retains more colour, flavour and vitamins.

Before dinner

Reduce the remaining 100ml of double cream on a low heat. Once reduced, top each ring of dauphinoise with cream and place into the oven to heat through with the lamb on a separate covered tray. Heat the spinach in a pan with a small amount of butter, and do the same with the mushrooms using a little oil.

To plate

Place the dauphinoise at the top of the plate and spread the spinach below. Slice the lamb or leave the fillets whole and place on top of the spinach. Scatter mushrooms around the plate and finely chop some rosemary to garnish all over. If desired, you can serve a light lamb jus with the dish.

The Ubiquitous Chip
LAMB NECK, AUBERGINE PURÉE, ARTICHOKE, ROAST TOMATO

The Ubiquitous Chip has become a byword for Glasgow cooking, in more ways than one. This is not the kind of place you can just build; it has to develop over time. The restaurant and brasserie is as much a product of the efforts of the talented staff as the genial atmosphere generated by its faithful cadre of bohemian customers who come here to tell stories and eat modern Scottish dishes.

Preparation time: 15 minutes | Cooking time: 40 minutes | Serves: 4

Ingredients

1 large aubergine

12 cherry tomatoes

Pinch of salt and sugar

10ml lemon juice

50ml extra-virgin olive oil

Pinch of white pepper

1 tbsp baby capers

4 1.2kg portions of lamb loin

6 baby artichokes, cooked and halved

100ml lamb gravy

To serve:

8 pitted black olives, thinly sliced

50g feta cheese, crumbled

Watercress leaves

Method

If you have a gas hob, cook the aubergine carefully over the flame, turning occasionally, allowing the skin to char and blacken until tender. This will impart a smoky flavour to the purée and greater depth of flavour to the dish.

Preheat the oven to 200°c. Lightly oil the aubergine and place on an oven tray on the top shelf of the oven for about 45 minutes, or until cooked through. Reduce the oven temperature to 180°c. While the aubergines are cooking, halve the cherry tomatoes and place them in a small pan. Toss in a little olive oil, salt and a pinch of sugar then cook for 4 minutes until softened slightly.

Carefully scrape the flesh from the aubergine skins, combine it with the lemon juice and olive oil and blend until smooth, adding a little water if necessary to make a loose purée. Season with salt and white pepper to taste.

Deep fry the capers at 180°c until crisp then set aside on kitchen paper to drain. Season the lamb then sear all over, basting the lamb in the fat as it renders down. Transfer to the preheated oven for 30 to 35 minutes for medium rare, or longer if you prefer. Toss the artichokes in oil and salt and warm through at the same time. Gently heat the lamb gravy and aubergine purée. Allow the lamb to rest while you assemble the dish.

To serve

Spoon the aubergine purée onto the plates, carve the lamb loin into three even-sized pieces and arrange along the purée. Place the artichokes and tomatoes around the lamb. Scatter some olive slices and feta cheese over the plates. Finally, spoon over a little lamb gravy and garnish with the crispy capers and watercress leaves.

Madha Indian
NALLI GOSHT

Madha owner Joseph K. Joseph is from Kerala in the southwest of India where they are blessed with an abundance of spices – cardamom, black pepper – and an enviable supply of fresh fish. The people of north India prefer dishes with nuts, cream, roti naans, vegetarian stews and paneer cheese. His authentic restaurant brings together all these contrasting flavours on Albion Street. We've picked out this recipe, a traditional favourite served at formal dinners from Kashmir to Hyderabad.

Preparation time: 10 minutes | Cooking time: 40 minutes | Serves: 2

Ingredients

For the lamb:

Baby leg of lamb on the bone

1 potato

1 large carrot

2 onions

2 tomatoes

50g French beans

1 tsp salt

3 mace blades

10g bay leaves

1g green cardamom

1 tsp cloves

1g black cardamom

2 tsp freshly grated garlic

2 tsp freshly grated ginger

Pinch of ground turmeric

2 green chillies

10g black peppercorns, crushed

For the garnish:

Fresh ginger

Coriander leaves

Method

Put all ingredients except the garnish into a pot and pour over enough water to cover the lamb. Slow cook it until the lamb is soft and tender.

Remove the lamb from the gravy once it's cooked well. Boil and reduce the gravy to a thick sauce then blend it well and strain it.

Serve the lamb on a deep dinner plate and pour the sauce over it. Garnish with matchsticks of ginger and coriander leaves.

Bilson Eleven
LOCH ETIVE TROUT SASHIMI WITH VERDITA SAUCE

Head chef Nick Rietz tells us: "Like all good dishes, the idea for this was first touched upon in a bar. Max's on Queen Street do a verdita that is a traditional sidecar to a good sipping tequila. The verdita is so vibrant and clean it pairs brilliantly with raw fish. You can also swap the trout for salmon in this recipe. For a wee twist you can cure the fish in a tequila marinade which also works well."

Preparation time: 20 minutes | Serves: 4

Ingredients

200g trout (get your fishmonger to take off the skin and pin-bone the fillet)

For the verdita sauce:

50g fresh coriander

50g fresh mint

½ jalapeno, deseeded

500ml pineapple juice, from concentrate

2 ice cubes

Pinch of xantham gum (optional)

Method

Double check the fish for any remaining bones, and then slice into roughly half centimetre portions.

For the verdita sauce

Blend the coriander, mint, jalapeno and pineapple juice with the ice cubes. If you want the sauce a little thicker, you can add a pinch of xantham gum which is available from most food shops.

Pass the sauce through a sieve and either pour around the fish or transfer into a separate bowl for dipping.

There should be plenty of verdita sauce left over for a round of tequila or two afterwards!

Café Gandolfi

BLACK PUDDING WITH MUSHROOMS AND PANCAKES

Seumas MacInnes, owner of Café Gandolfi, tells us: "There's a standing joke amongst my staff that I am on a ceaseless quest for new recipes that include black pudding. The following is one of my enduring favourites. Stornoway black pudding is a simple, homely food but it has delighted me for years with its distinctive, zesty taste and generous adaptability."

Preparation time: 15 minutes | Cooking time: 10-15 minutes | Serves: 8

Ingredients

1 onion, finely chopped

Drizzle of olive oil

200g button mushrooms, sliced

2 cloves of garlic, finely chopped

½ glass of white wine

1 tbsp sherry vinegar

Salt and freshly ground pepper

16 slices of MacLeod & MacLeod Stornoway Black Pudding

For the pancakes:

200g self-raising flour

Pinch of salt

2 eggs, beaten

2 tsp maple syrup

50g caster sugar

140ml whole milk

50g salted butter, melted

Method

First, sauté the onion in olive oil on a low heat until transparent. Add the mushrooms and garlic, cook for 5 to 7 minutes then add half a glass of white wine and the sherry vinegar. Cook for a further 5 to 7 minutes to get all the flavours working together. Season to taste.

Place the slices of black pudding into the preheated oven and cook for 10 minutes, turning over after 5 minutes.

For the pancakes

Sift the flour with a good pinch of salt. Add the eggs and then the rest of the ingredients, beating until a smooth consistency is achieved. Heat a non-stick frying pan over a low to medium heat.

Once the pan is hot, start to make your pancakes, keeping them fresh and warm by wrapping them in a clean dish towel.

To serve

For each person place two pancakes on a warm plate, top with two slices of black pudding, add a tablespoon of the mushroom mixture and enjoy!

This is THE PLAICE

A'Challtainn are purveyors of piscine delights and one of the coolest places to eat in the city.

Stride through the gates to The Barras at The Calton entrance and take a left beside the curious building made from shipping containers, the only new building added to the famous market complex in the last 40 years. The courtyard here has become home to artists, performers and street food at weekends.

It's all part of the swagger acquired by the Barras Art and Design Centre, which has found a renewed sense of purpose as the venue for an outstanding restaurant and bar.

Promoters Ricky Scoular and Brian Traynor, sensing a burgeoning appetite for the best Scottish seafood and a rising East End, opened here in 2016 amid much fanfare and the occasional raised eyebrow.

Success has followed. For starters, expect dishes like scallops with garden pea, pancetta and truffle oil or a simple plate of chilled prawns; the best of Scotland's sea harvest.

You'll also find various lobster dishes, often served with a shovelling of salty, hand-cut chips. A suitably Glaswegian preparation for the king of crustaceans.

"We're upping the ante on the service and whole general experience in here, but still keeping it as a relaxed atmosphere" Brian Traynor told us. "We want people to come in and realise that you can still have top quality service, great local produce, good imaginative cooking, ideas throughout the menu, but also a much more laid-back environment. It's very accessible to anybody and everybody."

A'Challtainn have forged strong links with their suppliers, deliveries of sustainably sourced seafood and local meat and vegetables fuel their creative cooking. A bold menu has reconnected this part of the city with the wider Glasgow food scene and provided new reasons to look east for your next dinner reservation.

A'Challtainn

A'Challtainn
PLAICE AND CLAMS WITH GRAPEFRUIT EMULSION

Our Plaice is sourced sustainable from Shetland. Oven baked, our simple, classic flavours of plaice and cockles allow the produce to speak for itself. Topped with this buttery, rich and vibrant grapefruit emulsion makes this dish a real showstopper. The perfect blend of classic and fresh just like us!

Preparation time: 10 minutes | Cooking time: 40 minutes | Serves: 4

Ingredients

Salt and pepper

4 medium-sized plaice

30ml olive oil

50g butter

3 large slices of pink grapefruit

For the clams:

500g clams

100ml white wine

2 cloves of garlic

1 large shallot

For the grapefruit emulsion:

Nage from the clams

2 pink grapefruits, juice

Chives, finely chopped

20g brown sugar

Salt

20g butter

To serve:

Sea vegetables, raw

Method

Preheat the oven to 220°c. Oil a baking sheet large enough to accommodate the plaice. Season the surface of the baking sheet and place the fish on it, pale side (underside) down. Drizzle the fish with olive oil and massage it in. Season all over with pepper and lots of salt and dot the little pieces of butter over it. Lay three large slices of grapefruit on top of the fish and bake for 20 to 30 minutes, until the fish is just cooked.

Serve whole or if you wish, once roasted, the flesh of the plaice should lift easily from the bone in neat fillets. Remove the top two fillets using a fish knife and fork. Ease the skeleton away to reveal the remaining two fillets from the underside.

For the clams

Place the clams in a medium-sized pot and steam together with the white wine, garlic and shallots. Once the clams have opened remove them from the pot and strain the juices.

For the grapefruit emulsion

Place the leftover juices from the clams in a medium-sized pot, add the grapefruit juice, chives, brown sugar and a pinch of salt and reduce to one third. Stir in the butter in small amounts until the emulsion forms.

To serve

Serve the plaice whole on the plate with the clams on top, sea vegetables on the side and surrounded by the grapefruit emulsion.

The Mediterranean LIFESTYLE

Enjoy friendly hospitality and international flavours when you dine in three contrasting restaurants: Alla Locanta, Sannino's and Da Luciano

For a true taste of Italian and Mediterranean cooking in your own kitchen, try the recipes for Linguine Frutti Di Mare, Gnocchi Da Luciano and Sultan Kebabs on the following pages. These fantastic signature dishes showcase the style of cooking from three restaurants that you should visit for yourself.

Alla Locanta is a restaurant committed to delivering an authentic Mediterranean dining experience. Found on Pitt Street in the heart of the city centre, the modern décor keeps it bright and fresh during the day, with cosy soft lighting at night.

Alla Locanta is just round the corner from the King's Theatre and a five minute walk from Theatre Royal Glasgow, Charing Cross Rail Station and the Buchanan Street shops. Their two course lunch menu offers excellent value for money, with dishes including hot and cold meze, barbecued swordfish from the grill or penne pasta.

Nearby, Sannino's offers a little taste of Italy in a modern, lively restaraunt, popular with the theatre crowd and nearby office workers. The menu boasts authentic Italian cuisine made with fresh and locally sourced ingredients. Popular dishes include the cappesante piccolo with Shetland king scallops, Italian sausage, lemon butter and rocket or the house speciality, misto alla griglia with grilled mini fillet steak, chicken breast and Italian sausage and truffle oil mashed potato.

Da Luciano is an inviting Italian restaurant and wine bar on Bothwell's Silverwells Crescent. Alongside a bar lounge, the bright, modern dining room has a popular sun terrace. The lunch and pre-theatre menu includes dishes such as minestrone soup, pizza and rigatoni with chestnut mushrooms and a spinach and cream sauce. The set prestige menu introduces delicious choices like scallops from the Isle of Barra, veal saltimbocca and fillet steak with a peppercorn sauce.

If The Glasgow & West Coast Cook Book has inspired you to try new flavours and enjoy some of the best cooking in the west, visit Alla Locanta, Sannino's or Da Luciano for top hospitality.

Alla Locanta
SULTAN KEBABS

The fusion of a Turkish and an Italian restaurant, housed in the same premises, allows diners to enjoy a heady mix of Mediterranean and meze style dishes in this popular, family-run place on Pitt Street. Choose from Italian pizzas and pasta or Turkish small plates. This kebab dish is a favourite of the kitchen.

Preparation time: 2 hours | Cooking time: 20 minutes | Serves: 2

Ingredients

For the kebabs:

100g chicken breast

8oz fillet steak

100g lamb fillet

100g lamb mince

2 lamb chops

For the kofta seasoning:

1 clove of garlic, finely minced

¼ small onion, finely minced

½ tbsp parsley, fiinely chopped

1 tsp tomato purée

1 tsp chilli pepper paste

For the marinade:

Salt and black pepper

1 tsp oregano

1 tsp chilli pepper paste

Olive oil

1 tsp yoghurt

For the rice:

250g basmati rice

2 tbsp unsalted butter

Salt and pepper

500ml water

For the salad dressing:

2 tbsp pomegranate molasses

1 tbsp lemon juice

½ tbsp Dijon mustard

3 tbsp olive oil

Salt and pepper

To serve:

Chilli peppers

Tomatoes

Garlic sauce

Chilli sauce

Method

For the kebabs

Cut the chicken, steak and lamb fillets into even cubes with a large, very sharp knife and add to a skewer.

Combine the lamb mince with the kofta seasoning in a large bowl, form into cubes and add to a skewer.

Mix all the marinade ingredients together and apply to the cubed chicken, lamb and beef skewers and the lamb chops. Use enough olive oil to effectively cover the meat in the marinade. Leave for 2 hours in the fridge.

Barbecue the meat over charcoal. 6 minutes should do. We recommend cooking the lamb and beef to medium and making sure the chicken and kofta is thoroughly cooked through.

For the rice

Place rice into a bowl with enough water to cover. Set aside to soak for 20 minutes and then drain.

Heat up a large pot till scalding and add the butter, salt and black pepper before adding the drained rice. Cook and stir the rice for a few minutes until the rice is lightly toasted.

Pour in the water and bring to the boil. Once boiling, reduce the heat to low, cover and simmer for about 15 minutes, or until all of the water has been absorbed. Let stand for 5 minutes, then fluff with a fork before serving.

For the salad and dressing

The salad can be prepared while the meat is marinating using whatever fresh vegetables you like. We use lettuce, red bell peppers, rocket, red cabbage, red onions, cherry tomatoes and carrots.

To make the dressing for the salad blitz together all the ingredients for 20 seconds in a blender.

To serve

Place the salad on one half of the serving platter with dressing drizzled over the top, then place the rice on the other half of the platter. Grill the chilli peppers and tomatoes then place these with the meat skewers, koftas and lamb chops around the platter.

Serve with garlic and chilli sauce on the side.

Da Luciano
GNOCCHI DA LUCIANO

Da Luciano offers a signature mix of Italian and Scottish cuisine in the heart of Bothwell. A family favourite, the menu features pasta, pizza and grill dishes.

Preparation time: 5 minutes | Cooking time: 25 minutes | Serves: 1

Ingredients

1 hen's egg

2 slices of Parma ham

100g potato gnocchi

Knob of butter

2 courgette flowers

6 spring onions

Method

Place the egg in a cold pan of oil on a low heat to fry until cooked. Bake the Parma ham at 120°c for 20 minutes. Bring a pot of water to the boil then blanch the potato gnocchi until it floats. Drain the gnocchi and quickly fry in a pan of hot melted butter until crispy, then drain again. Blanch the courgette flowers in boiling water for 30 seconds. Either chargrill the spring onions and courgette flowers or use a blow torch. Combine the gnocchi with the spring onion and courgette flowers, add the Parma ham crisps and put the fried egg on top.

Sannino Pizzeria
LINGUINE FRUTTI DI MARE

Treat yourself to the fruits of the sea
with this simple and satisfying pasta recipe.

Preparation time: 5 minutes | Cooking time: 12 minutes | Serves: 2

Ingredients

For the Napoli sauce:

Drizzle of olive oil

1 small onion, chopped

½ red pepper

½ carrot

3 tomatoes, chopped

½ small bunch of basil

Sea salt and black pepper

For the linguine and seafood:

200g linguine

Dash of olive oil

100g king prawns

50g calamari

50g mussels

5g onions, chopped

5g fresh chillies

5g peppers, chopped

Dash of white wine

Method

For the Napoli sauce

Add a touch of olive oil with the onion, red pepper and carrot to a saucepan, caramelise it for about a minute then add the chopped tomatoes, and half a glass of water. Bring to the boil and add basil, then cook for a further 2 minutes. Season with sea salt and black pepper, then blend it all together and leave the sauce to cool.

For the linguine and seafood

Bring a pot of water to the boil and add the linguine. Add a touch of olive oil to a hot pan. Place the king prawns, calamari and mussels in the pan and stir well. Add the onions, chillies and peppers, then cook until caramelised. Add a dash of white wine and season with sea salt and black pepper. Stir well. Add your Napoli sauce and allow to simmer for 5 minutes.

To serve

Combine the pasta with the seafood sauce and stir well. Serve with a garnish of your choice; we use parsley and Parmesan shavings.

Kelvingrove's
TASTE OF ITALY

Baffo Pizza and Birra on Argyle Street, right across the road from Kelvingrove Art Gallery, is home to the Mezzo Metro pizza in Glasgow and open seven days a week to eat in or take away.

Back in 2015, Baffo's owner and founder, Francesco Longo, was on a trip to Verona with his family and quickly fell in love with a little pizza place at the end of the road serving Italy's finest by the metre and so plans to open something similar back in Glasgow began. His family has Italian blood, with roots in the south of the country, so it felt like a natural thing to do. In the middle of 2016, Glasgow welcomed Baffo to the local food scene.

Francesco sourced several pizzaiolos from his family's hometown in Italy and brought them to Glasgow to start working on Baffo's signature style pizza. He wanted to make sure that his customer's experience was as authentic and delicious as possible and with a background spanning over 20 years in hospitality, he had the staff and the skills to open a great pizzeria.

Using only the freshest ingredients, sourced locally and from Italy, the dough is proved for 48 to 72 hours, then hand-stretched and cooked in an Italian pizza oven for 60 to 90 seconds at over 400°c. This creates a combination of a perfectly blistered pizza crust, the best sugo and the right amount of toppings to balance the flavour.

The team at Baffo takes pride in their food and work to create a relaxed atmosphere in the restaurant. In addition to pizza, you can also find a selection of street food sides, cut to order antipasti, focaccia, traditional and modern bruschetta and of course a selection of pasta to rival nonna's. And let's not forget the family favourite, Tiramisu.

Baffo Pizza

Baffo Pizza & Birra
TIRAMISU: A FAMILY RECIPE

Baffo owner Francesco Longo says: "This recipe has been passed down the generations. My nonna used to visit us every year from the South of Italy, where my dad was born and raised, and would take over the kitchen in our house to cook a whole host of dishes from sweet to savoury. Naturally, she passed on several recipes to my mum and dad who then passed them on to my sister and I. I have tweaked the recipe slightly to make it mine, but it's the same ingredients and method, I just build it differently. However you make your Tiramisu (meaning "pick me up"), make sure the coffee is strong!"

Preparation time: 30 minutes plus 2 hours setting time | Cooking time: 10 minutes | Serves: 8

Ingredients

4 double espressos

250g mascarpone

300ml double cream

4 large eggs

150g caster sugar

Savoiardi biscuits (otherwise known as ladyfingers)

8 jam jars

Cocoa powder, to serve

Method

Prepare the four double espressos and place in a shallow dish. Put the mascarpone into a bowl and soften it by mixing, then slowly add the double cream and whisk together until it has the consistency of a thick whipped cream. Separate the eggs and whisk the whites on high speed or vigorously by hand while slowly adding in 50g of sugar until the mixture becomes a fluffy, soft peak. Slowly whisk the remaining sugar into the egg yolks over a low heat until pale and frothy then gently fold into the mascarpone mix.

Dip the sponge fingers into the coffee until they are nicely soaked, but not soggy. Layer a few into each jam jar at the bottom about two centimetres high, don't be afraid to squish them in a bit. Then fill the rest of the jar with the mascarpone mixture. Repeat eight times until all the jars are full.

Cover and chill for anything from a few hours to overnight and you can keep it in the fridge for up to 2 days. When you are ready to serve them up, sprinkle the cocoa powder over the top and serve to your guests.

Pizza PARTY

Basta Disco Pizza Bar. That covers most of it. This Partick hangout has an adventurous approach to cooking.

The foundation of the menu at Basta is imported Polselli flour, Strianese tomatoes and extra-virgin olive oil from Italy. Plus fresh produce sourced as close to home as possible, including from the local Sandy Road Community Garden. After that, anything goes. No flavour combination is considered too outlandish. If it works, it's on the menu. Meanwhile, Prince or Chic is usually on the stereo. They want to bring the joy back into pizza with interesting toppings and an easy-going vibe in the dining room.

Chef owner Jane Chalmers says: "We serve fairly traditional pizzas on the menu but the more popular ones are the specials that we work on in the kitchen. Our first special was 8 hour Irn Bru ham and fresh pineapple, finished with a blow torch. It was our version of a Partick Hawaiian.

"We like to experiment. Our recipe in this book, for example, it all started with a chat in the kitchen. My partner's dad was coming in for his 85th birthday and he loves Cullen Skink, so I came up with this pizza, and he was delighted, even though it's a bit odd. We hope people will give it a try at home.

The small team at Basta are masters of their art and that gives them the confidence to take things up a notch in the kitchen. Jane wrote the menu but she wanted their range to keep evolving. "One of the great things about doing food like pizza is that you are able to express yourself and that's really caught the imagination of our customers too."

Often regulars will ask for their own topping combinations "or sometimes people come in and just ask for something spicy," Jane says with a laugh.

The word basta means 'enough' in Italian. "Basically, myself and Innes, my business partner, we've been in the industry for a long time, and we've always worked for other people. We decided we'd had enough of that and wanted to work for ourselves." They've found their niche, serving up pizza from their super-heated oven, joining a cadre of other independent businesses making Dumbarton Road a cooler place.

Basta
CULLEN SKINK PIZZA

Surprising and outrageously tasty, try a pizza recipe that expertly fuses elements of Italian and Scottish cooking. Combining ricotta sauce, cooked potato pieces and smoked haddock for a pizza less ordinary, the Basta gang reveals the secret behind this innovative Partick comfort food.

Preparation time: 35 minutes | Cooking time: 8-10 minutes | Makes: 4 pizzas

Ingredients

For the dough:

500g 00 flour

10g fine sea salt

300ml lukewarm water

4g dried instant yeast

2 tbsp olive oil

For the cullen skink:

100g ricotta cheese

200ml double cream

Salt and pepper

200g undyed smoked haddock

Milk

3 bay leaves

10 peppercorns

1 small onion

50g butter

1 medium potato, diced into small cubes

To assemble:

2 x 125g packs of mozzarella pearls

100g Applewood smoked cheddar, diced into small cubes

To finish:

Chives, chopped

Extra-virgin olive oil

Method

First of all, choose your soundtrack. We recommend a mixture of Grandmaster Flash, Chic, Prince, The Lijadu Sisters and Sister Sledge but it's really up to you.

For the dough

Make the dough by placing the flour and salt into a large mixing bowl and mixing together. In a jug mix together the water, yeast and olive oil using a whisk and set aside for a couple of minutes.

Slowly add the yeast mixture to the flour, bit by bit, and mix together using your fingers until you have a sticky dough. Leave to sit in the bowl for about 15 minutes and then turn out onto a well-floured surface and knead for about 10 minutes until you have a much smoother ball of dough.

Place into an oiled bowl, cover with a cloth or cling film and leave to rise for a few hours until doubled in size. Turn the dough out and knock the air out of it then cut into four equal sized pieces. Make each piece into a dough ball by pulling dough out and pushing into the middle, then turn the dough 45 degrees and repeat until you have a smooth, round ball. Put the balls onto a floured plate and set aside for at least half an hour before cooking.

For the cullen skink

Mix the ricotta and cream together with a fork until smooth and add salt and pepper to taste.

Poach the haddock fillets in enough milk to cover the fish with the bay leaves and peppercorns. Once the milk boils remove from the heat. Remove the haddock fillets and flake into pieces.

Cut the onion in half and slice very thinly. Melt the butter in a pan and add the onions. Cook over a very low heat until soft but not browned.

Boil the potato pieces in salted water until tender and strain.

To assemble

When you are ready to make the pizzas preheat your oven to its highest setting, about 250-260°c.

Take each dough ball and stretch out gently using your fingers until it is about 30cm in diameter. You can roll them out but stretching gives a better texture. Place on a baking tray or pizza tray if you have one.

Top the pizza with a few large spoonfuls of the ricotta cream mixture and spread it out over the base leaving a rim of about two and a half centimetres around the edge. Then add the cooked onion, evenly distributing slices over the ricotta sauce. Repeat with the cooked potato pieces and smoked haddock. Scatter the mozzarella pearls and smoked cheddar cubes evenly over the top.

Bake in the oven until the dough is browned and the toppings are bubbling. This should take about 8 to 10 minutes but keep an eye on it as temperatures may vary from oven to oven. Finish by scattering over some chopped chives and a drizzle of extra-virgin olive oil. Serve and enjoy.

Southside SPECIAL

A family run Continental restaurant with a strong Italian spirit and a Glaswegian heart.

Built as a particularly exotic looking tram station in 1915, this Southside landmark fell into a state of disrepair before being rescued in a restoration led by Marco Giannasi, who opened an Italian bistro here in 1994. He bought the building from the council for one pound and spent two years meticulously creating what has become a much-loved local restaurant.

The interiors are sophisticated and gloriously traditional. The rooms seem bigger on the inside than they do on the outside. It's like taking a step into a self-contained Glasgow culinary bubble where service is prompt and warm, conversation flows as easily as the wine, people relax and linger over their meal.

You'll find familiar pasta Bolognese, carbonara or arrabiata. Signature dishes include a linguine frutti di mare seafood blend of west coast mussels, prawns, Fort William farmed salmon, squid sautéed with fennel, chilli and garlic white wine sauce.

"The chef, Marino, that opened the restaurant is still here after 24 years. He is still strong and fit and demanding quality and high standards. He works with Tony, the manager, who has been here as well since we opened. They were there for the beginning of the story," owner Marco says with a smile.

The redevelopment of the old Victoria hospital site beside Battlefield Rest will bring new people to the area, but Marco says he still sees the same customers coming year after year.

There's a consistency to the cooking and some enduring dishes on the menu but they like to play around with things in the kitchen too. Experiments like their haggis cannelloni proved popular.

"We like to source the best Scottish produce, and I also independently buy pasta products, prosciutto and salami from the North of Tuscany," Marco explains. "My family has roots in Tuscany so I like to keep that connection. You can have the best of Scotland and the best of Tuscany in the Southside of Glasgow. Customers appreciate we are trying to do new things and pick up new ingredients to keep the menu alive."

Marco says he now sees customers that started coming to Battlefield Rest as children returning as adults with their own children. "They come back now they are big boys and girls. The restaurant still has a charm for them. They bring their families. We have that kind of relationship with customers, it's an emotional connection that makes the restaurant special, beyond the meal and the atmosphere. They leave their troubles at the door and talk to us, we counsel them and they counsel us. It's that kind of place."

Battlefield Rest
SMOKED HADDOCK RISOTTO WITH STORNOWAY BLACK PUDDING AND CRISPY EGG

A dish that matches the character of Battlefield Rest, this risotto dish is ideal for sharing with friends. Bring the flavours of the Southside's favourite Italian bistro to your own kitchen with this simple recipe.

Preparation time: 20 minutes | Cooking time: 25 minutes | Serves: 4

Ingredients

For the risotto:

50g butter

1 onion, chopped

1 clove of garlic, chopped

250g Arborio risotto rice

50ml dry white wine

1 litre fish stock

2 leeks, finely sliced

300g smoked haddock

Salt and pepper

50g Parmesan, freshly grated

For the crispy egg:

4 free-range eggs

50g flour

1 egg, beaten

100g panko breadcrumbs

For the black pudding:

4 slices of Stornoway black pudding

For the garnish:

50g rocket

Drizzle of olive oil

Method

For the risotto

Heat the butter in a heavy-based saucepan, then add the onion and garlic. Fry gently until the onion softens and goes transparent. Add all the rice, mix in well with the butter, onion and garlic, then fry while stirring for 45 seconds. Add the white wine and stir for a further 30 seconds, then add the fish stock.

Bring your risotto to the boil and cook for 5 minutes, stirring all the time, then turn the heat down to a simmer for a further 10 minutes, while continuing to stir.

Add the leeks and smoked haddock to the risotto mix and gently cook for 5 more minutes until the rice is cooked through. Season, then add Parmesan and take off the heat.

For the crispy egg

Boil the eggs for 5 and a half minutes, then cool them down and take off their shells. Dip the egg in flour, then in the beaten egg, then the breadcrumbs and set aside.

Deep fry the egg for 1 minute then season.

For the black pudding

Place the black pudding slices under a preheated grill and cook for 3 minutes on each side.

To serve

Time to bring it all together. Place a slice of black pudding on a plate. Add some of the risotto on to the black pudding and then place a small bunch of rocket on the pile. Cut the egg in half and then place on top. Drizzle with oil and serve.

Deli life in
LENZIE

Sue and Mark Billington opened an award-winning deli in Lenzie in 2012 that has since become a focal point for the local community and a platform for small food producers. Both have come from a hospitality background; Mark had ran restaurants in Glasgow and Sue had worked in catering on and off since she was 15 years of age. The opportunity to set out on their own came when they spotted the vacant shop and decided it was the right time for them.

The recipe they feature in this book started as a conversation with a customer looking to purchase an Italian cheese. "I managed to source the cheese for her through one of my suppliers," says sue. "I loved the cheese so much, so asked her for the recipe she was using, which has become a firm family favourite."

"The shop has become the hub of the community. Everybody meets here," Sue explains. "Folk meet up for a birthday drink, or just to catch up with friends or family over lunch or dinner. Grandparents come in with the grandchildren for an ice cream and a coffee. It means we have lots of regular customers and we talk to them a lot about the food they want to eat."

There are also regular social events in the deli, with wine, gin and whisky clubs. There's also a pudding club for those who just love dessert. The café is open every day for lunch and food in the evening, with a large selection of beers, wines, gins and prosecco by the glass or beer on tap.

The Billingtons have recently developed their own Lenzie Gin, which has taken its inspiration from the cranberries and bilberries that grow wild on the moss, a local preservation area where people like to walk.

People regularly come into the shop asking if they can help source ingredients, often from around the world. One of the key elements of the Billington family's place is the space it offers to small artisan producers. "I like to find things that you won't see in the supermarket. Look at our shelves and you'll see local fudge, tablet, chocolate or biscuits, anything that really excites me."

Their fresh daily bread comes from a local baker and is made from an old sourdough recipe that has been handed down. They make all their own homemade quiche, pasta and soup. For quirky ingredients and independent flavours, make your way to Lenzie.

Billington's of Lenzie
BAKED CHICKEN WITH ITALIAN TALEGGIO CHEESE AND PESTO

This chicken dish is a favourite Billington family dinner. This recipe was kindly given to them by a valued customer after she came into the deli to ask if they sold Taleggio cheese. They ordered some in for her and for themselves. They have since added their own twist to the recipe.

Preparation time: 10 minutes | Cooking time: 40 minutes approx. | Serves: 6

Ingredients

6 skinless and boneless chicken breasts

Salt and ground black pepper

175g Italian Taleggio cheese cut into small cubes straight from the fridge. You can use mozzarella cheese if Taleggio isn't available.

3 tbsp fresh pesto (homemade if possible)

3-4 tbsp full fat cream cheese

80-100g homemade breadcrumbs. Stale focaccia rolls or sourdough loaves are good for this

Grated Parmesan cheese to taste

2 punnets cherry vine tomatoes

Large bunch of fresh asparagus, trimmed

Olive oil

Method

Preheat oven to 200°c/180°c fan.

Place the chicken breasts in a shallow ovenproof dish. Season each breast with salt and pepper. Place the cubed Taleggio cheese, fresh pesto and cream cheese in a mixing bowl, and mix well together.

Spread the mixture over each chicken breast covering them completely. Sprinkle over the breadcrumbs and then top with Parmesan cheese. Bake for 20 minutes.

Place the cherry tomatoes and trimmed asparagus in the baking tray around the chicken. Drizzle over olive oil, and season with salt and pepper to taste. Bake for a further 10 to 15 minutes. Be careful not to overcook or burn the breadcrumbs.

Plate each chicken breast with a few tomatoes and asparagus spears. Spoon over any juices and serve with sautéed potatoes.

Catch of THE DAY

A neighbourhood restaurant that's attracting attention from across the country for serving exceptionally sourced seafood, cooked to perfection.

The idea arrived fully formed: to "open a high end, quality fish and chip experience. One that shows off the seafood of Scotland". As Giancarlo Celino grew up, his family had fish and chip shops before selling up and going into the wider restaurant industry. Like many of us, he retains fond memories of this glorious Glasgow dish. This was the inspiration to open his own restaurant.

You can find Catch on Fenwick Road in Giffnock. They also have a home delivery shop on Clarkston Road, Netherlee and have just opened their biggest restaurant yet on Gibson Street in Glasgow's West End. In three years of business, there has been a tremendous response as Catch has worked to elevate fish and chips to an art form.

Giancarlo explains: "I thought there was a real gap in the market. Everyone loves fish and chips so why not have the best? No-one can beat Scottish seafood, so I wanted to include lobster, haddock and scallops, all with fantastic chips. It's been a roaring success since we first opened the doors."

The restaurant has caught the attention of the critics. In the first year, Catch was recommended in the Michelin Guide. In 2017, they were named in the top 10 independent restaurants in the UK by the National Fish & Chip Awards.

Everything in Catch is cooked to order and served in a casual, stylish nautical themed restaurant. "We want the freshest fish possible. Our motto is 'from shore to door in 24' and we want to stick to that with all our seafood. It will be landed at the harbour and then on your plate within a day," Giancarlo says, enthusiastically. Typically, the fish is landed at Peterhead where it is processed and then arrives at Giffnock for 6am and is cooked for lunch.

Signature dishes include half lobster with garlic butter, gourmet scampi, smoked haddock or fish finger sandwich, which are all served with a generous portion of twice-cooked chips. You can also expect halibut, langoustines, sea bass and lemon sole.

Giancarlo feels they are delivering a modern take on traditional, much-loved dishes. "We've brought fish and chips back, and that's exactly what we wanted to do. We have reminded people of how good these dishes can be."

Continuing to look to the future, Catch plans to open in the city centre in 2019.

Catch
LOBSTER ROLL

The main ingredient in this dish is fresh Scottish lobster. We chose this dish to showcase our great local produce in an international favourite.

Preparation time: 15 minutes | Cooking time: 20 minutes | Serves: 2

Ingredients

1 Scottish lobster

1 celery stick, finely diced

2 tsp cayenne pepper

6 tbsp mayonnaise

½ lemon, juice only

2 x 6 inch long hot dog buns

10g butter

½ iceberg lettuce, chopped

2 radishes, finely sliced

Pea shoots

Method

First, bring a deep pan of salted water to the boil. Add the lobster and cook for 7 minutes per half kilogram of weight. (So a 1 kilogram lobster would need 14 minutes.) Once cooked, plunge the lobster into iced water and reserve until needed.

Remove all of the white meat from the lobster.

Mix together the diced celery, cayenne pepper, mayonnaise and lemon juice.

Open both hot dog buns and lightly toast. Butter both sides of the buns. Add the chopped lettuce and the mayonnaise mixture to the inside of the buns. Place the lobster meat on top. Before serving, add sliced radishes and pea shoots to garnish.

What a GUY

A man for all seasons, Guy Cowan draws on a broad palette of flavours to create dishes to delight the senses. He's one of the best known personalities on the Glasgow food scene.

Guy Cowan was never one of those children who had to be cajoled into eating. "I have had a passionate love affair with my lunch ever since I was able to use my cutlery to prevent raiding siblings from pillaging my vittles," he says. Guy's grandfather was well known Glasgow grocer John Curley, he tells us, as he begins to talk about his food background. "It was ham and eggs. Blocks of butter. It was always good, hearty, tasty solid food."

Embracing new cuisine wherever he could find it growing up, he went on to open a deli in the West End during the late 80's; "I was ahead of my time." Then came more than 25 years feeding the film and music industry's A-list with his location catering business. Jon Bon Jovi said he made a "rockin' red pepper sauce", Mick Jagger gave him a handwritten thank you note and Ken Stott entrusted him with his mother's recipe for Caponata.

Eventually, Guy decided that living out of a suitcase was "best left to younger chefs" and headed home to Glasgow. In Guy's Restaurant on Candleriggs he created a wonderfully unconventional place, with a menu rooted in Scotland, but open to international influences. Nowhere else in the city can you eat sushi, sashimi, mince and tatties, steak tartare or a variety of homemade ravioli at one table.

Having divested his interests in the restaurant, one of Glasgow's biggest food personalities is looking at a future of dining pop-ups, catering commissions and food collaborations. It's an exciting time for a talented chef and local character.

He has an eclectic approach to cuisine. "There's a big Italian influence on my cooking, but very much Asian food as well. I've been eating and cooking Japanese food for a long, long time. I remember there was only one Japanese food shop in the whole of Scotland, it was on Costorphine Road. I like taking traditional recipes and then changing them. Particularly Scottish dishes."

We ask him about his approach to cooking. There's a long pause. "I've always maintained, everything should taste good." Warming to the subject, he goes onto explain, "I'm fed up going into places where you are served a dish that looks absolutely stunning, but it tastes of nothing. Whether it's a pea on the side of the plate or it's the main centrepiece of the meal, it should taste good! You need to come up with the goods!"

é Pasta e Basta

SQUID INK TAGLIOLINI WITH KING SCALLOPS AND MONKFISH

A favourite recipe of Guy's, combining flavours from Scotland and Italy, this eye-catching dish aims to impress.

Preparation time: 40 minutes | Cooking time: 20 minutes | Serves: 4

Ingredients

For the pasta:

225g 00 flour

75g semolina

3 whole eggs

1 egg yolk

2 tsp squid ink

1 tsp extra-virgin olive oil

2 tsp hot water

For the sauce:

Half white onion, finely diced

2 large cloves of garlic, finely chopped

Chillies, any type – any amount to your own taste

Extra-virgin olive oil

½ lemon, juice only

200g monkfish fillet, cleaned and cut into scallop sized pieces

8 king scallops, cleaned and roe removed. You can the add roe to the sauce if you wish

Salt flakes and freshly ground black pepper

Spring onions, roughly chopped, white and green separate

1 lemon, zest only

Handful flat leaf parsley, roughly chopped

Method

For the pasta dough

Make a mound with the flour and semolina, then make a hollow in the middle for the eggs, yolk, squid ink, olive oil and water. Gently mix the eggs with a fork drawing in a little flour bit by bit. Once the liquid has been absorbed use your fingers to mix all the flour into a dough.

Alternatively, put all the dough ingredients in a food processor and blitz until thoroughly mixed.

Whatever method used, the next step is to knead the dough by hand for about 10 minutes, then wrap in cling film and refrigerate for at least 30 minutes. If your dough is too dry add a little water, if too wet add a little flour. You could make this the day before.

After the dough has rested, scatter some semolina flour on a board and cut the dough into four pieces, covering three lumps with cling film. Flatten the dough you are about to work with by hand then, using a rolling pin, roll the dough before passing it through your pasta rolling machine open at its widest setting.

Fold the dough over on itself and pass through the rollers again. Now going down a number with each pass roll the dough until thin, I find setting seven or eight on the machine ideal.

Cut your dough in sheets approximately 20 to 25cm long then put through the tagliolini cutter on your machine. Dust with semolina and either hang on a pasta drying rack or lay out on a pasta drying tray. A clothes horse works perfectly. Repeat with the remaining three balls of dough.

For the sauce

Soften the onion, garlic (and chillies if using) in olive oil over a medium heat. Once the onions are opaque add the lemon juice and reduce. Next drop in the monkfish and stir, coating in the oil. Now add the scallops (and roe) salt, pepper, and white spring onion, stirring frequently. Finally add the lemon zest, parsley (keep some for decoration) and green spring onions.

While the sauce is cooking, just after adding the fish, place tagliolini in a pot of salted water at a rolling boil. This should cook in about 2 minutes if still fresh or up to 5 minutes if dried.

Drain the pasta, reserve a dessert spoonful of the cooking water and add to the sauce. Add the pasta to the sauce pot and toss in the fish making sure every strand is coated.

Serve in deep bowls scattered with chopped parsley and black pepper.

é Pasta e Basta

HAND-CUT PAPPARDELLE WITH BEEF FILLET & CHERRY TOMATOES

Hand made pasta is a lot easier than you think. Give this recipe a try, you'll be glad you did.

Preparation time: 20 minutes | Cooking time: 40 minutes | Serves: 4

Ingredients

For the pasta:

225g 00 flour

75g semolina

3 whole eggs

1 egg yolk

1 tsp extra-virgin olive oil

2 tsp hot water

For the sauce:

1 white onion, finely diced

4 large cloves of garlic, finely chopped

Chillies, any type – any amount to your own taste

Extra-virgin olive oil

200g cherry tomatoes, halved

400g finest beef fillet steak (or sirloin if preferred) cut into cubes or thick strips

Salt flakes and freshly ground black pepper

Spring onions, roughly chopped, white and green separate

Handful fresh sage leaves, chopped

Handful flat leaf parsley, chopped

Parmesan, grated

Method

For the pasta dough

Make a mound with the flour and semolina, then make a hollow in the middle for the eggs, yolk, olive oil and water. Gently mix the eggs with a fork drawing in a little flour bit by bit. Once the liquid has been absorbed use your fingers to mix all the flour into a dough.

Alternatively, put all the dough ingredients in a food processor and blitz until thoroughly mixed.

Whatever method used, the next step is to knead the dough by hand for about 10 minutes, then wrap in cling film and refrigerate for at least 30 minutes. If your dough is too dry add a little water, if too wet add a little flour. You could make this the day before.

After the dough has rested, scatter some semolina flour on a board and cut the dough into four pieces, covering three lumps with cling film. Flatten the dough you are about to work with by hand then, using a rolling pin, roll the dough before passing it through your pasta rolling machine open at its widest setting.

Fold the dough over on itself and pass through the rollers again. Now going down a number with each pass roll the dough until thin, I find setting seven or eight on the machine ideal.

Cut the dough in to sheets approximately 20 to 25cm long then using a festooned or smooth pasta cutting tool (or sharp knife) cut into broad ribbons. Dust with semolina and either hang on a pasta drying rack or lay out on a pasta drying tray. A clothes horse works perfectly. Repeat with the remaining three balls of dough.

For the sauce

Soften the onion, garlic and chillies in olive oil over a medium heat. Once the onions are opaque add the tomatoes and cook, stirring frequently. Now add the beef, salt, pepper, and white spring onion, stirring frequently. Finally add sage, parsley (keep some for decoration) and green spring onions.

While the sauce is cooking, just after adding the beef, place pappardelle in a pot of salted water at a rolling boil. This should cook in about 2 to 3 minutes if still fresh or up to 5 to 6 minutes if dried.

Drain the pasta, reserve a dessert spoonful of the cooking water and add to the sauce. Add the pasta to the sauce pot and toss in the ragu making sure every strand is coated.

Serve in deep bowls scattered with masses of Parmesan, chopped parsley and black pepper.

Power to the PEOPLE

The team at The Fish People Café are united by one thing: a passion for seafood, wine and hospitality. They believe that no dish can be better than its ingredients, and that the best ingredients are usually local.

When Andy Bell and family looked at the adjacent industrial café to their southside fishmongers that had lain dormant and disused for a number of years, they saw an opportunity. Seizing the chance to try something new, they embarked on a substantial renovation of the neighbouring unit. Resplendent in the French bistro décor that you see today, the doors opened on The Fish People Café in September 2012.

The restaurant team are led by head chef John Gillespie and manager, Graham Hamilton. "Both are experts in their field with John working as a chef for 30 years and Graham working front of house for 32 years," explains Laura Bell. "They have been with us since we opened six years ago and are the foundations of the restaurant."

John's cooking style consists of simple, classic dishes with an Asian twist, showcased in their featured tandoori sea bass recipe shared in this book and another customer favourite : steamed sole fillets en papillote with Asian greens and sesame. The menu consistently features the finest Scottish seafood, including Tarbert landed monkfish, Cumbrae rock oysters, which can be enjoyed at the marble oyster bar, Campsie Glen smoked salmon and hand-dived Barra scallops.

John's food philosophy centres on offering high quality sustainable fish at affordable prices. All fish is sourced from their very own fishmongers. "Our retail shop is next door to the café and we also have a wholesale unit in the East End which supplies Glasgow and the surrounding areas. As a wholesaler we pride ourselves on providing the highest quality of fresh seafood and have a loyal customer base that will testify to this," Laura says.

They also use local suppliers such as Seasonal Produce for their fruit and vegetables, J.R. Fine Foods for cheese and dairy and Thorntonhall for ice cream.

The Fish People Café is a small but dynamic restaurant with a changing seasonal menu. Customers are an eclectic mix of locals and visitors to the city. "We are a bit of a destination restaurant, with an unusual location, so it means all the more when customers travel to see us. Many of the customers are regulars and know the staff well. Graham ensures that everyone is greeted warmly and that the high standard of service never slips."

The Fish People Café
TANDOORI SEA BASS

The Fish People Café offers a modern twist on classic seafood dishes that showcase the finest fresh fish and shellfish that Scotland has to offer, all carefully sourced from their very own neighbouring fishmonger

Preparation time: 20 minutes | Cooking time: 20 minutes | Serves: 4

Ingredients

4 whole sea bass (400–450g each)

For the tandoori paste:

375g natural yoghurt

10 cloves of garlic, peeled

60g fresh root ginger

5 tbsp sunflower oil

5 tbsp fresh lemon juice

55g paprika

2½ tsp each of garam masala, turmeric, chilli powder, cumin and salt

For the curry oil:

2 onions, roughly chopped

10 cloves of garlic, chopped

100g root ginger, peeled (keep the peelings as they can go into the oil)

1 cinnamon stick

1 tbsp garam masala

3 tbsp curry powder

1 tbsp turmeric

200g tomato purée

500ml sunflower oil

500ml extra-virgin olive oil

100g fresh coriander

1 tsp salt

For the samphire pakora:

100g gram flour

¼ tsp each of crushed coriander seeds, ground cumin, salt, turmeric and chilli powder

Pinch of baking powder

150g samphire

Method

Ask your fishmonger to gut, scale and score the flesh of the sea bass on each side. This allows the tandoori paste to get into the flesh of the fish. You can make the curry oil and tandoori paste ahead of time as they can be kept in the fridge in sealed containers for 4 to 6 weeks.

For the tandoori paste

The tandoori paste is very easy to make. Just place all of the ingredients into a jug blender or liquidiser and blend until smooth.

For the curry oil

In a heavy-based saucepan pour in the sunflower oil and sweat off the onion, garlic and the finely diced peelings of the root ginger for 5 minutes. Add the cinnamon stick and the garam masala, curry powder and turmeric then cook for a further 2 minutes. Add the tomato purée and olive oil and simmer at a low heat for 25 minutes ensuring it doesn't stick, then set aside to cool slightly. After cooling, pass the oil through a mesh sieve and discard all the pulp.

Line a seive with muslin or a J-cloth and place it over a clean bowl. Pour in the oil and let it drip through, then set aside to cool completely.

Chop the coriander and blend this and the salt with the curry oil. Finely dice the peeled root ginger and add to the cooled curry oil

For the samphire pakora

Mix all of the pakora ingredients except the samphire in a bowl and add enough water to make a thick batter. Add in the samphire and set aside.

For the sea bass

Season the whole bass with salt, fry in a hot pan for 1 minute on each side then place on a metal oven tray. Spread each fish with a generous amount of tandoori paste and bake in the oven at 220°c for 8 to 10 minutes.

Place small batches of pakora mix into a deep-fat fryer at 180°c for 3 to 4 minutes until crisp and golden brown.

Place a bass on each serving plate, drizzle with the curry oil and place under a hot grill for 1 minute to warm the oil.

Serve the cooked fish with the pakora on the side and mini poppadoms, basmati rice and fresh lemon.

Country LIFE

Fruin Farm is set in the tranquil surroundings of Loch Lomond and The Trossachs National Park. Visit for exceptional locally-sourced food prepared by head chef Paul Moran and enjoy the great outdoors.

Fruin Farm is a restaurant set in the foothills of Loch Lomond, a 40 minute drive from Glasgow. The country setting, with llamas, rare breed sheep, goats, guinea fowl, ducks and pigs allows customers to enjoy fine food in an area of outstanding natural beauty. Visit for a farmyard tour, a llama trek, or a culinary journey that highlights some of the best ingredients Scotland has to offer.

"Our food is simple", says owner Wayne Cleworth, "the dishes are uncomplicated, yet the balance of flavours and ingredients makes for a very bold statement, one which is hard to put into words and which is so much easier to understand if you just come and try our food."

They're living the rural idyll up at Fruin Farm, rearing their own pigs, cultivating a small herb garden which their chefs dip into. They take wild garlic to make the most incredible pesto. Iain Butcher, a retired biochemist, makes all of Fruin Farms jams from fruit he grows locally in Alexandria. Callaghan of Helensburgh and Puddledub in Kirkaldy supply their meats, while the hens of Townhead Farm supply them with free-range eggs and all their milk is organic. A lady called Jackie and the Beanstalk at Carman Hill in Renton grows organic vegetables, which features regularly on each of their menus.

They begin the day by making their own bread, cakes and scones and go on from there, till they get to Friday and Saturday nights' "unpretentious fine dining" as they like to call it.

"At Fruin Farm we never stand still," exclaims Wayne, referring to both the hard-working ethos of their small but dedicated kitchen and front of house team and the fact that he and co-owner Rebecca have a one year old baby who has just learnt to walk. "Our menu, like ourselves, is in constant motion. Our menu evolves throughout the day, from breakfast through to dinner, each month and, indeed, with the seasons, ensuring only the freshest of produce makes it into our chefs larder and on to the plate each day."

A meal at Fruin Farm could start with ginger-braised pig's cheeks, butternut squash purée and honey roast baby golden beetroot, continue with herb crusted coley, gnocchi, wild mushrooms, truffle oil, then finish with cinnamon rice pudding, roast apples, pears and cranberries for dessert. A true taste of the country.

Fruin Farm
GINGER BRAISED PUDDLEDUB PIG'S CHEEKS

The secret to the succulence of this dish is cooking the cheeks low and slow.
You don't need an AGA for this dish... but it certainly helps!

Preparation time: 30 minutes | Cooking time: 2-3 hours | Serves: 4

Ingredients

For the braised pigs cheeks:

8 Puddledub pork cheeks (trimmed of any sinew)

Salt and pepper

3 tbsp olive oil

2 large banana shallots, diced

1 carrot, diced

4cm piece of root ginger, diced

Bouquet garni

1 star anise

½ tsp coriander seeds

½ tsp fennel seeds

330ml can ginger beer

750ml chicken stock

For the butternut squash purée:

1 butternut squash, diced

Sprig of thyme

Sprig of rosemary

Piece of Parmesan rind

1 tbsp olive oil

100g unsalted butter

100ml double cream

10g Parmesan, grated

Salt and pepper

For the glazed beetroot:

4 baby golden beetroot

1 tsp olive oil

1 tsp honey

Salt and pepper

Method

For the pigs cheeks

Heat a large, deep saucepan, season pork cheeks with salt and pepper, spoon two tablespoons of olive oil into a pan, add the cheeks one at a time and caramelise both sides, remove cheeks from pan and set aside.

Add the remaining olive oil, the shallots, carrot, ginger, bouquet garni, star anise, coriander and fennel seeds to the same pan and cook until golden brown. Add the ginger beer and reduce by two thirds. Place the cheeks back into the pan.

Pour in chicken stock to cover the cheeks, bring to the boil then reduce to a simmer. Slowly cook for 2 to 3 hours or until tender (when cooking, make the purée and cook the beetroot at this point). Once done remove the cheeks and keep warm.

Pass the cooking liquor through a sieve into a clean saucepan and reduce to a thick glaze, add the cheeks back at this point and cover in the reduced sauce.

For the butternut squash purée

Tie the thyme, rosemary and Parmesan rind together. In a large saucepan bring the oil and butter to a foam, add the squash, herbs and rind, cover and cook slowly until soft. Remove the tied herbs, blend the cooked squash with the double cream, grated Parmesan, and salt and pepper then keep warm until serving.

For the glazed beetroot

Place the beetroot in a small saucepan, cover with water, add a pinch of salt, bring to the boil and cook for 8 minutes. Take off the heat and leave to cool in the water. Once cool enough, peel the beetroot with a paring knife and half lengthways. Heat the oil in a small frying pan and seal the beetroot cut side down, add the honey then season.

To plate

At one side of the serving plate spoon a generous amount of squash purée in a pile. Drag the serving spoon through the purée to the opposite side, place the cheeks and a little sauce along the purée, place the beetroot in between and finally garnish with micro coriander and red amaranth.

Fresh IS BEST

Chef patron, Derek Marshall, spent much of his early career honing his skills in Europe, developing a passion for sourcing and cooking regional produce on a culinary adventure that would take him to the Channel Islands, the French Alps and Spain.

Inspired and motivated by his time working abroad, Derek returned home to Glasgow with a new appreciation of fresh, seasonal ingredients and a clear plan to showcase Scotland's incredible natural larder.

"Back in 1998 when I came up with the concept for Gamba, I always believed that by using the freshest produce and keeping things honest, simple and consistent, we'd have the perfect recipe for success."

Now in it's 20th year, Gamba has gone from strength to strength, winning multiple awards and maintaining two AA Rosettes for two decades. Derek's principles have paid off and letting the superior quality ingredients take centre stage has proven to be a winning formula.

You get a sense it is a serious operation as soon as you arrive. The smart, efficient staff. The plush surroundings. The heft of the wine list.

The inherent seriousness of a proper, grown-up restaurant is moderated by that Glasgow commitment to informality. Occasional bursts of loud laughter, the hum of conversation and bonhomie assure you that you can have fun here.

"Gamba has always been about quality and consistency; you can't fool Glaswegians and right from the start I knew that everything I did would have to be transparent."

Using only the highest quality fish and seafood, Derek's team combine classic techniques with a modern twist to create picture-perfect plates with inspired flavour combinations, delivering the honest, consistent and memorable dishes synonymous with Gamba.

As much as the simple, honest cooking mantra is the defining principle of the menu, there are regular flourishes that demonstrate commitment to technique and flair. An unexpected Asian influence catches the eye.

"Our dishes are generally quite simple because my philosophy in the kitchen has always been to let the ingredients shine. We focus on the impeccable sourcing of our produce and allow the food to speak for itself."

Derek and the team at Gamba are fully committed to sustainability, making it the perfect spot in Glasgow to enjoy the fruits of the sea completely guilt-free. Their foup – fish soup with Portland crab meat, stem ginger and coriander – has become the signature dish of the restaurant.

Gamba

Are you looking for the bar, Fly?

Gamba
FOUP WITH PORTLAND CRAB MEAT, STEM GINGER AND CORIANDER

A true Gamba classic and our most sought after recipe. This rich, Asian-inspired fish soup can be a meal in itself, with a steaming bowl providing the ideal comfort food for seafood lovers.

Preparation time: 45 minutes | Cooking time: 45 minutes | Serves: 6

Ingredients

Fish stock (makes 3-4 pints):

1.8kg fish bones (turbot, lemon sole or monkfish are best)

1 tbsp vegetable oil

1 onion, finely chopped

1 leek, finely chopped

½ whole bulb of garlic, sliced horizontally

2 litres water

1 lemon, sliced

2 sprigs of parsley

For the fish soup:

50g unsalted butter

2 medium onions, chopped

4 cloves of garlic

50g ginger

75ml brandy

3 tbsp plain flour

3 tbsp tomato purée

1.15 litres fish stock

450g white crab meat

50g grated stem ginger

1 packet fresh coriander, chopped

150ml rapeseed oil

Maldon sea salt

Ground white pepper

Method

For the fish stock

Wash the bones thoroughly and cut into chunks where possible. Put the oil in a warm pan and cook the vegetables and garlic for a few minutes. Do not allow to colour.

Add the chopped fish bones and cook without colouring for about 5 minutes. Add the water and bring to the boil. Skim well, removing any froth.

Add the lemon and parsley and simmer for 20 to 30 minutes. Pass through a sieve and leave to cool. Once cool, the stock can be frozen and stored for use later. If stuck for time, try using a quality off the shelf fish stock that you can pick up from the supermarket.

For the fish soup

Melt the butter over a low heat in a thick-bottomed pan. Chop the onions, garlic and root ginger, and sweat in the butter. Add the brandy and reduce.

Mix in the flour and cook for about 5 minutes, still on a low heat. Add the tomato purée and keep mixing. Start adding fish stock little by little, mixing all the time. Add the white crab meat and cook for 30 to 40 minutes.

Liquidise the soup, and pass through a sieve into a clean pot or bowl. Add the grated stem ginger and some of coriander. Then, liquidise the remaining coriander with the rapeseed oil. Lightly drizzle the coriander mixture onto the soup to garnish. Season and serve in warm bowls.

A Finnieston FEAST

A highly regarded stalwart of the Glasgow restaurant new wave, The Gannet has attracted international attention for their innovative approach to fine dining in a modern, casual setting.

Ivan Stein and Peter McKenna escape from the kitchen to take a seat in The Gannet's dining room. Lunch service is finished and they have a short period of calm before guests start arriving for dinner. They are working chefs and owners: preparing dishes, organising ingredients, devising menus.

Ivan is from London, Peter is Irish and worked across Europe and the Mediterranean. Both gravitated towards Glasgow. They couldn't see a restaurant they wanted to work in. So they created their own in a vacant tenement building that had been derelict for almost a decade. With the help of some architects and a significant amount of hard work, a stylish bar and restaurant was fashioned from the space.

The concept for the restaurant was born in the summer of 2012 on a trip to the Hebrides to source produce for their kitchen in the West End. By the end of the trip, they had met scallop divers, oyster growers, fishermen, smokers, farmers, game producers and some interesting characters. "We've put the time in," Peter says. "We've spent countless days travelling around Scotland in the the car, going to farms, visiting gamekeepers we had heard about.

"Now, there isn't a main ingredient in the restaurant that doesn't come directly from the source. Every two weeks we get a side of beef, for instance. I know the farm that it comes from, what it's been grazing on. We have total control over the product."

The menus are dictated by the rhythms of the seasons. The relationships the chefs have with local producers, combined with their flair in the kitchen, are the basis of their success. As if to prove the point, a farmer walks in the door with some pig's heads to sell. Downstairs there is a sack of huge wild Scottish mushrooms from a forager they work with. Conversations and direct engagement with the people who cultivate the best produce will guide the kitchen. "Recipes evolve and techniques in the kitchen change to a certain extent, but I know I'll be cooking with venison, duck and high quality Scottish seafood for as long as this restaurant's here," Ivan says.

Restaurant manager Kevin Dow adds another important dimension to The Gannet story. He has an easy manner, quick wit and a great knowledge of ingredients and wine to share. The front of house staff are natural hosts. A meal here in Finnieston is among the very best culinary experiences in the city.

The Gannet
SWEET CICELY CURED HERRING

Peter and Ivan from The Gannet have chosen to share a recipe from their own kitchen, a quintessentially Scottish dish of layered flavours, easy to prepare at home as a snack.

Preparation time: 2 weeks | Serves: 4-8

Ingredients

For the pickled herring:

8 herring

30g salt

30g sugar

Sprig of sweet cicely leaf

200ml white wine vinegar

80g sugar

1 bay leaf

3 black peppercorns

1 juniper berry

3 fennel seeds

3 coriander seeds

Pinch of mustard seeds

2 sweet cicely pods

½ small sweet onion

½ small carrot

For the horseradish crème fraîche:

50g crème fraîche (use best available, we use The Wee Dairy Dalry)

5g grated horseradish

Lemon juice

Sea salt

For the pickled cucumber:

¼ cucumber

50g sugar

50ml white wine vinegar

30ml water

1 clove

½ bay leaf

1 white peppercorn

Method

For the pickled herring

Fillet the herring and trim, then cure overnight in salt, sugar and sweet cicely leaf. Make a pickling liquor by heating the vinegar, sugar and add all the spices. Allow to cool. Slice carrots and onions thinly on mandoline. Rinse the herring then layer with the onions and carrots and pour the liquor over the fish. Leave for a minimum of 2 weeks in an airtight container.

For the horseradish crème fraîche

Mix the crème fraîche with horseradish, season with the lemon and sea salt, then hang in muslin for 4 hours.

For the pickled cucumber

Peel the cucumbers and cut out the centre with a cutter, then slice it thinly. Dice the outsides. Dissolve the sugar in the liquids then add the clove, bay leaf and white peppercorn. Chill then vacuum pack with the cucumber.

To serve

Arrange some cucumber pickle in the centre of the plate, add the pickled herring (removed from the liquid) and top with a dab of the horseradish crème fraîche.

From farm TO PLATE

A warm Glasgow welcome and relaxed hospitality greet you as the kitchen brings together meticulously sourced produce at this charming neighbourhood restaurant.

Mhairi Taylor's family have had a strong influence on her food philosophy. Her grandfather was known as Zique – his real name was Donald MacGregor – and she has fond memories of him singing the traditional Scottish song, MacGregor Gathering, at meal times. So, when she opened the bakery by Zique she transformed the space beside her much-loved Cafezique into a produce-led restaurant, there was a particular thought that she kept returning to.

"My husband Dick Lewis is a farmer – most of the meat we use is supplied by his farm, next to Monachyle Mhor hotel. My son, Johnny, has become a shepherd, even though he is an out-and-out Glaswegian. The pair of them are always talking about gathering produce or the animals. I like the idea of bringing ingredients and people together, uniting great staff. That became the story of this place and I gave my head chef Jamie Donald free rein in the kitchen. He makes great use of Scottish produce but the mother cuisine is Italian."

Gather by Zique has a focus on nose-to-tail eating: "we will have whole pigs and whole sheep, utilising everything apart from the oink and the baaa," Mhairi says.

Meanwhile, foraged vegetables and locally sourced fruit feature heavily in the seasonal menus devised by chef Jamie, previously of Gandolfi Fish, Jamie Oliver's Fifteen and Bocca Di Lupo. So vegans and vegeterians will be well catered for.

"I grew up on the top of a hill overlooking Loch Lomond. I was really privileged that we grew our own potatoes, or we grew peaches and nectarines in the greenhouse. I think I'm happiest out in the garden. We want to bring that colour and the light, fresh flavours of nature into our restaurant," Mhairi says.

Gather by Zique has taken up the mantel of a prized neighbourhood eating place. "We've been here for 17 years on this street. We've met regular customers and their children have been born and grown up coming to us, now they are off to university. We've really got to know folk and we're part of the community."

The stylish dining room has a typical West End setting on Hyndland Street but it is emphatically linked to the Scottish countryside through the kitchen's respect for the ingredients that are allowed to shine in smart, beautifully presented dishes. "We cook the stuff we want to eat, to create the restaurant that we want to go to," Mhairi says. Try the lamb recipe from Gather by Zique and you will understand.

Gather by Zique
ROAST LAMB RACK WITH CELERIAC CAPONATA

A hearty dish, informed by European cuisines, our lamb dish is an excellent example of the restaurant's culinary philosophy.

Preparation time: 10 minutes | Cooking time: 30 minutes | Serves: 4

Ingredients

1 lamb rack, trimmed of all fat, allow 180–200g per person depending on appetite. Ask your butcher to do this and give you the fat/trimmings for rendering.

For the celeriac caponata:

50g raisins

100ml balsamic vinegar

1 large celeriac, or 2 small ones

2 red onions

1 head of celery

6 cloves of garlic

½ tsp dried chilli flakes

1 tsp chopped thyme

100g green olives, stoned and chopped

100g pine nuts, toasted

1 tbsp capers, chopped

50g parsley, roughly chopped

For the rosemary and anchovy dressing:

30g rosemary

1 clove of garlic

2 anchovy fillets

50ml olive oil

For the braised cavolo nero:

500g cavolo nero

2 cloves of garlic

½ dried chilli flakes

1 tbsp olive oil

Knob of butter

100g lamb fat

Method

Place the lamb fat in an appropriately sized saucepan with a little olive oil and cook on a low heat until there is a decent amount of fat in the pan. Strain through a sieve. Keep the fat and discard the solids.

For the celeriac caponata

Soak the raisins in the balsamic vinegar. Peel the celeriac, season with salt and pepper, slather in olive oil and bake in an oven preheated to 190°c for about 20 minutes. The outside should be golden and crispy and a small knife should penetrate to the centre with no resistance. Set aside to cool.

In a heavy-based pan on a medium heat, sweat the onions, celery, garlic, thyme and chilli flakes. When soft, turn the heat up a bit and stir while allowing the mixture to catch on the base of the pan but don't let it burn. Add the balsamic raisins and allow to boil and reduce in the pan. Add the chopped olives, toasted pine nuts, capers and parsley. Remove from the heat. When the celeriac is cool enough take a knife and fork and pull it apart into bite-size chunks. Add to the rest of the ingredients, mix thoroughly and set aside.

For the rosemary and anchovy dressing

Fry the rosemary in a little oil until crispy but maintains its colour. Drain and pulverise in a mortar and pestle with the garlic and anchovy. Add the olive oil, mix and set aside.

For the braised cavolo nero

Strip the cavolo from its stalks and blanch in plenty of boiling salted water. Remove from the water with a spider or slotted spoon, lay flat on a tray and drizzle with olive oil. Set aside until it's time to finish the dish. Keep a small cup of the cooking water.

To assemble

Having blanched the cavolo, rendered the fat, made the caponata and the dressing, now it's time to cook the lamb and assemble the dish.

Cook the lamb as a whole piece. In a large heavy-based frying pan, put two tablespoons of the rendered fat, one tablespoon of olive oil and a knob of butter. Heat the fats until they sizzle and add the lamb, seasoned on all sides with salt and pepper. Brown all sides of the lamb and then place in an oven preheated to 200°c.

Roast until it reaches a core temperature of 42 to 44°c depending on your oven, this could take anything up to 15 minutes. You could probe the meat after 5 or 6 minutes to assess the temperature and keep checking until the desired temperature is reached.

Remove from the oven and rest. This is very important as it will allow the juices in the meat to flow evenly and produce an end product with a beautifully even and pink colour. Rest the meat for half the time it took to cook.

Now, warm the caponata in a saucepan. In another pot lightly toast the garlic and chilli for the cavolo nero in the remaining rendered lamb fat, add the reserved cooking water and the cavolo and cook on a fairly high heat until the liquid has reduced and is coating the cavolo.

Put the cavolo and the caponata on the plate, cut the lamb to the desired size, plate and enjoy.

Making their
MAKAR

Glasgow Distillery's spirits are hand-crafted in three distinctive copper stills: Annie, Mhairi and Tara, each named after a family member of the three founding partners. Mike Hayward, Liam Hughes and Ian McDougall are pioneers of Scotland's new wave of single malt distilleries and proud crafters of Glasgow's first ever range of gin; the multi award-winning Makar Gin. Get to know the local favourite spirit with these tasting notes and cocktail suggestions.

Makar Original Dry Gin is a vibrant, juniper-led gin, handcrafted in small batches. Nose: invigorating fresh pine and eucalyptus, floral and herbal rosemary notes with touches of zesty lemon citrus. Palate: robust juniper supported by citrus and savoury notes, black pepper spice with hints of liquorice contributing to a fully rounded and balanced mouthfeel. Finish: long smooth dry finish, with notes of angelica and lingering warm pepper spice and rosemary.

Makar Oak Aged Gin is the award-winning cask matured variant of the Original Dry Gin. Matured in tailor-made virgin oak wood casks over 10 weeks, it has incredible colour, flavour and a distinctive smoothness derived from its maturation process. The nose: fresh pine and smoky oak, rosemary and citrus, mellowed by soft notes of baked vanilla, warm spices and cinnamon. The palate: bonfire toffee opens up the palate followed by soft juniper and herbaceous vanilla, with a hint of fresh coffee and dark chocolate. The finish: warming peppery finish with soft smoky undertones.

Makar Mulberry Wood Aged Gin adds another layer of complexity by ageing the Original Dry Gin in virgin mulberry wood casks. The nose: bright cassia spice complements a fruity charred wood aroma. The palate: waxy lemon with a hint of vanilla and white chocolate. Incredibly soft and surprisingly sweet on the tip of the tongue, with a nip of juniper and anise. The finish: incredibly smooth finish with a hint of sweet lemon and light pepper complemented by a fruity fresh spice.

Makar Old Tom Gin re-creates a traditional sweeter style of gin which is enjoying a renaissance. The nose: juniper opens up the nose before delicate floral notes lead to sweet honey and the delicate aroma of freshly chopped coriander leaves. The palate: liquorice, honey almond marzipan are balanced by herbaceous coriander with a black pepper spice. The finish: dry, crisp with a subtle lingering sweetness.

Makar Cherry Gin is a delicious fruit addition to the Makar Gin family. The nose: dried cherries and autumnal spice followed by fresh juniper with subtle hints of citrus & vanilla. The palate: ripe cherry and citrus lead to fruity juniper, spice and notes of stone fruits. Hints of liquorice lead to a smooth lingering finish of dried cherry and warming spice.

Makar Gin COCKTAILS

The Glasgow Distillery has invested in the world's best distilling equipment and assembled an innovative team of distillers to produce a range of premium spirits, including gin and single malt whisky. Sourcing the finest ingredients and casks from around the world whilst harnessing a natural water supply from Loch Katrine guarantees a range of products that stand out from the crowd.

Glasgow Distillery company has created their five-strong range of Makar Gin so that each sits perfectly at the centre of a gin-led cocktail, with each gin providing an entirely unique taste.

Makar Original Dry Gin: Classic G&T

Fill a highball glass with fresh ice. Measure and add 50ml of Makar Original Dry Gin. Top with a premium quality tonic water and garnish with a fine slice of fresh mild green chilli pepper.

Makar Old Tom Gin: Bee's Knees

Fill a mixing glass with fresh ice. Measure and add 50ml of Makar Old Tom Gin. Combine with 12.5ml of honey, 15ml of lemon juice and 25ml of orange juice. Stir the mixing glass thoroughly for 30 seconds, until the contents within are ice cold. Strain the contents of the mixing glass into a chilled cocktail glass and garnish with a twist of fresh lemon peel.

Makar Oak Aged Gin: Oak Negroni

Fill a mixing glass with fresh ice. Combine 25ml of Makar Oak Aged Gin with 25ml sweet vermouth and 25ml Campari. Stir the mixing glass thoroughly for 30 seconds, until the contents within are ice cold. Fill a rocks glass with fresh ice and strain the contents of the mixing glass onto the ice. Garnish with a twist of fresh orange peel.

Makar Mulberry Aged Gin: Mulberry Martini

Fill a mixing glass with fresh ice. Combine 50ml of Makar Mulberry Aged Gin with 15ml of dry vermouth. Stir the mixing glass for 30 seconds, until the contents within are ice cold. Strain the contents into a martini glass. Garnish with 3 olives.

Makar Cherry Gin: Cherry Collins

Fill a highball glass with fresh ice. Measure and add 50ml of Makar Cherry Gin. Combine with 15ml lemon juice, 15ml sugar syrup and top with soda water. Garnish with a fresh maraschino cherry.

Get yourself to THE GREEK

Looking to Athens for inspiration when it comes to food and drink, Halloumi brings a dash of Mediterranean sunshine to Glasgow.

Small plates, big flavours: that's the ethos of Glasgow's top Greek restaurant, Halloumi. With a wide selection of dishes infused with sunshine and the modern taste of the Mediterranean to choose from, it's like going on your holidays on Hope Street. Seasonal highlights include menu items like fiery dressed crab salad with avocado, chilli and spring onion or a tender swordfish steak with cherry tomatoes and speciality extra-virgin oil imported from Greece. Crumbly feta cheese and spinach make delicious crispy croquettes for vegetarians, as do the ever-popular halloumi fries, served with a layer of yoghurt, pomegranate, chopped mint and smoked paprika. There are plenty of meaty options on the menu too, including traditional slow-cooked stews, marinated lamb skewers and outstanding Greek flatbread kebabs or gyros.

The bar boasts a number of Scottish favourites alongside an impressive selection of Hellenic craft beer, Mediterranean wine and artisan Greek gin. While some of their eye-catching cocktails are named after Greek mythology, other crowd-pleasing creations are inspired by the breath-taking scenery of Athens – picture blooming wildflowers – which are perfectly Instagram-able and sure to please.

Lapreet Atwal, the general manager at Halloumi, explains Halloumi's approach to food: "Our dishes capture the essence of the Mediterranean spirit and culture – they're fresh, vibrant and big on flavour.

"Inspired by the beauty of Greece, our chefs want to offer the chance for our guests to sample exciting Hellenic flavours matched with drinks expertly created by our team. They cook everything to order using home-grown, locally sourced ingredients. It's Greek food, but nothing like you've tasted before. With our recipes, you can enjoy a taste of Greece in your own kitchen."

Halloumi is open seven days a week from noon until late, in a perfect spot for intimate dinners, catch-ups with friends, or a bite after shopping on the nearby Buchanan Street. The postcard blue décor and laid-back atmosphere will make you feel like you've stumbled across a hidden Greek oasis in the city. Their second venue Halloumi Southside has newly opened on Pollokshaws Road. Keep up to date with all things Mediterranean by following @HalloumiGlasgow and @HalloumiGlasgowSouth on Facebook and Instagram.

Halloumi

Halloumi SPANAKOPITA

"Spanakopita is a comforting dish that tastes great throughout the year," says Halloumi's head chef Muli Mukja. "For me, there's nothing better than the smell of freshly cooked layers of beautifully crispy spanakopita wafting through your kitchen. Perfectly baked Greek pastry smells delicious and tastes amazing with a light Greek salad."

Preparation time: 45 minutes | Cooking time: 45 minutes | Serves: 12

Ingredients

For the filling:

750g spinach leaves

3 bunches of spring onions

500g quality feta cheese

3 eggs

Large bunch of fresh mint leaves

Salt, to taste

Freshly ground black pepper

Nutmeg, grated

For the pastry:

Extra-virgin organic olive oil

Organic filo pastry, to complete 20 layers

1 egg, beaten

Method

About filo pastry

Filo pastry works best in the classic dish when it's thawed properly. It needs time to rest and too much moisture in the dough will end in disaster. Best to leave in the fridge for 12 hours before using. Then as you're getting ready to assemble, unroll your thawed sheets of filo and place between two slightly damp kitchen cloths to maintain temperature. This will also help the dough not to tear too much.

For the spanakopita

Preheat your oven to around 180°c. Wash and drain spinach thoroughly, and be sure to remove any excess liquid. Chop your fresh spinach leaves, spring onion and grate all the feta cheese into a large mixing bowl. Add your eggs, mint, salt, pepper and nutmeg to make the filling. Mix well.

Take a large baking dish and brush the sides with olive oil.

Line a flat tray or baking dish with two sheets of filo letting them cover the sides of the dish. Brush lightly each layer with an egg wash (take an egg and whisk in a small bowl).

Repeat until you have ten layers complete. Now, take the spinach filling and evenly spread the spinach and feta filling over the filo crust.

Continue to layer the filo two at a time, until you have ten layers on top of the filling each lightly brushed with an egg wash. Don't worry if the filo tears. Try and keep two of the best sheets for the top. Brush the very top layer with olive oil, and sprinkle with just a few drops of water. This will help it golden. Fold the flaps or excess from the sides, you can crumble them a little. Brush the folded sides well with olive oil. Cut the spanakopita only part way through into squares. Bake at 180°c for around 45 minutes until pastry is golden.

Bibimbap
KOREAN FRIED CHICKEN

Bibimbap on West Nile Street takes its name from Korea's favourite comfort food. Expect fresh, authentic Asian dishes on a menu featuring kimchi, noodles, deopbap and this outstanding fried chicken recipe. Visit for cocktails, sake and beats at the weekend.

Preparation time: 5 minutes | Cooking time: 10 minutes | Serves: 1-2

Ingredients

For the chicken with marinade:

4 skinless, boneless chicken thighs, quartered

½ yellow onion, grated

4 cloves of garlic, minced

1 tsp fine salt

½ tsp freshly ground black pepper

For the batter:

¾ cup cornstarch

¼ cup self-raising flour

1 tsp white sugar

½ tsp ground black pepper

¼ tsp salt

1 cup very cold water

Oil

Method

Grab a mixing bowl and stir together the grated onion, minced garlic, fine salt, and black pepper to make your marinade. Marinate the chicken by coating completely.

Cover the bowl with plastic wrap and refrigerate for at least 4 hours. If you can, leave overnight to get the most flavour into the chicken. Heat some oil in a deep-fryer or large saucepan to 171°c. Whisk the cornstarch, flour, sugar, salt and black pepper, and ¼ teaspoon salt together in a large bowl. Gradually whisk in the ice cold water until the mixture resembles a smooth pancake batter. Transfer chicken to the batter and stir to coat the chicken completely.

Working in batches, cook the chicken in preheated oil for 4 minutes. Transfer cooked chicken to a cooling rack. Increase oil temperature in the deep-fryer or large saucepan to 190°c. Working in batches, cook the chicken again in hot oil until golden brown and crispy on the outside, 3 to 4 minutes. Transfer to a wire rack to drain. You can enjoy this Korean fried chicken with a sauce of your choice, the spicier the better.

Pickled Ginger
VOLCANO ROLL

Go to Pickled Ginger, at the Finnieston end of St Vincent Street, for sushi, broth, bento and speciality temaki. Find the best cuisine of the east in the west of the city along with Japanese whisky and sake. Enjoy trying this recipe for a taste of their best selling Volcano Roll.

Preparation time: 5 minutes | Serves: 1

Ingredients

Half a sheet of nori (paper-thin toasted sheets of seaweed)

100g sushi rice, cooked

40g Scottish salmon

3 slices of avocado

5ml eel sauce

5ml mayonnaise

5ml spicy mayonnaise

5ml sriracha hot chilli sauce

1g sesame seeds

Method

Take the half sheet of nori seaweed and place it shiny side facing down. Spread out the 100g of cooked sushi rice to cover the whole sheet evenly. Carefully flip that over. Add three slices of avocado down the middle. Add two thin strips of salmon, about 40g. Roll it up.

Take one long crabstick and chop it finely the long way and put it on top of the roll. Put the sushi mat on top of your roll and give it a small squeeze to bind the crabstick to the roll.

Lift the mat and cut the roll in six pieces. Drizzle with mayo, spicy mayo and eel sauce and a sprinkle of sesame seeds.

Rioja
SUCKLING PIG WITH IBERIAN CHORIZO AND HAM

Rioja is a lively Spanish tapas restaurant and bustling late-night cocktail bar.
Enjoy modern Spanish dishes inspired by the Basque Country using the best
ingredients, from Galician beef to freshly caught Scottish seafood.

Preparation time: 24 hours | Cooking time: 48 hours | Serves: 10

Ingredients

For the suckling pig:

2 French racks of suckling pig, on the bone

Salt

1 sprig each of thyme and rosemary

4 cloves of garlic

1 cinnamon stick

Grapefruit and orange zest

For the suckling pig sauce:

15kg suckling pig bones

2kg onion

1.5kg celery

1kg leek

10 cloves of garlic

2 sprigs of thyme

30g tomato purée

500ml red wine

100ml sherry wine

100ml cane honey

50g butter, cubed

For the apple & cinnamon compote:

5kg red apples

1kg brown sugar

50g unsalted butter

3 cinnamon sticks

100ml white wine

For the patatas a lo pobre:

1kg Golden Wonder potatoes

Iberian chorizo

Cured Iberian ham

200ml of white wine

1 tsp smoked paprika

1 tsp thyme

Method

Preheat a water bath to 72°c. Season the French racks with salt, place the herbs, garlic cinnamon and fruit zests on the meat, then put both racks in a large vacuum bag. Seal with a bar sealer and cook in the water bath for 28 hours.

After this time, remove the French racks from the bag and drain. Remove herbs, fruits, garlic and cinnamon, and all the bones. Roll up the the piece of meat with the skin outside. Press and wrap with cling film and keep in the fridge for 24 hours.

For the suckling pig sauce

Roast the suckling pig bones on a tray in the oven for 1 hour 30 minutes, or until caramelised. Then add all the vegetables and roast for 2 hours all together.

Place the bones and the vegetables in a large pot. Heat the tray you were using and add the wine, the tomato purée and the cane honey. Scrape the tray to take all the juices and add them to the pot. Cover with water and bring to a simmer then cook for 36-48 hours, topping up with more water during cooking at least twice.

Pass the sauce through three layers of muslin cloth into a clean pan and add the sherry wine. Bring to the boil and reserve a small amount, then reduce by two thirds to reach a sauce consistency.

For the apple & cinnamon compote

For the apple and cinnamon compote, roast the apples with all the ingredients in the oven at 140°c for 3 hours. Then place all together in a Thermomix or similar and mix for 5 minutes at maximum power. Filter and then keep ready to serve.

For the patatas a lo pobre

For your patatas a lo pobres, peel your potatoes and cut them in brunoise, to a finely chopped mix. Do the same to thechorizo and ham. Place a large saucepan over a medium heat and add a splash of olive oil. Fry the meats softly, then add the potatoes and cook for 5 minutes. Add the thyme, white wine and smoked paprika, and place it in the oven until potatoes are cooked thoroughly.

To serve

Cut a portion from the suckling pig roll, about 110g, and fry in olive oil at a high heat, around 170°c, until the skin is crispy and golden. Place on kitchen paper to remove grease and oil. Pour some light sauce, not reduced, in the centre of the plate for a mirror effect.

Place the patatas a lo pobre on the plate, in a ring. Add the roasted apple compote on the side. Put a generous piece of suckling pig over the potatoes. Reduce the sauce with a bit of butter and finish with the sauce, some garlic, micro herbs and a few flakes of salt over the meat.

The French
CONNECTION

The menus at La Bonne Auberge offer excellent value for money and tantalising cuisine inspired by France and the Mediterranean.

In Glasgow, there are certain places that should be considered as gastronomic markers: restaurants that connect to a point in the culinary story of the city. One of the few still an active part of the food scene – La Bonne Auberge Brasserie – opened its doors on Bastille Day, 14th July 1975 and has been a proud AA Rosette holder since 1997. When it launched in Glasgow, La Bonne Auberge was hailed as a real step forward, thanks to the calibre of its wholesome and flavourful cooking, and over the years, it has continued to blaze the trail for other openings around the city. As Glasgow's original Mediterranean Brasserie, it captured the mood of the time and attracted the city's fashionable crowd. Since then, Maurice Taylor, founder of La Bonne Auberge, has become one of the most important local names in hospitality, winning a plethora of accolades and international recognition along the way, topped only by a well-earned CBE for his services to business and to charity.

Today, the multi-award winning La Bonne Auberge continues to flourish from its prominent location on West Nile Street, neighbouring the award-winning Holiday Inn Theatreland hotel. Executive head chef Gerry Sharkey, who has been leading the kitchen for over 25 years, has put his own stamp on the menus, while encouraging a progressive, forward-looking spirit in the kitchen and offering a range of French Mediterranean dishes at excellent value for money.

Guests can choose from a wide range of options including signature dishes such as boeuf bourguignon, corn-fed chicken supreme, monkfish, king prawns and of course, rib eye and fillet steaks. A variety of seasonal vegetarian dishes are always on offer and include a delicious pumpkin and ricotta pasta with roquette and herb butter. Whatever you order, save space for a delightful range of desserts – the crème brulée is highly recommended!

Surrounded by some of the city's top theatres including King's Theatre, Theatre Royal and Pavilion Theatre, as well as Glasgow Royal Concert Hall, La Bonne Auberge is the ideal spot for pre- and post-theatre and à la carte dining. The restaurant continues to serve as a salon for the thriving acting and cultural communities with long-standing links to many of the city's leading theatrical groups.

With over 40 years of experience, La Bonne Auberge remains a hugely popular choice for those celebrating special events, however there's no need to wait for an occasion. With its casual all day dining menu, La Bonne Auberge is the perfect choice for an informal catch up with friends over a tasty meal, always made to order using only the freshest, locally sourced ingredients and served by friendly staff in relaxed and inviting surroundings…..every day of the week!

La Bonne Auberge

CONFIT DUCK, CREAMED CABBAGE, SMOKED BACON, PINE NUTS AND POTATO ROSTI

La Bonne Auberge continues to thrive under the guidance of award-winning Executive head chef Gerry Sharkey.

Preparation time: 15 minutes | Cooking time: 3 hours 30 minutes | Serves: 2

Ingredients

For the confit duck:

2 duck legs

For the herb salt rub:

Handful of rock salt, 2 cloves of garlic, sprig of thyme, 2 bay leaves and a sprig of rosemary, all blended together

250g duck fat

For the mirepoix:

50g each of small diced carrots, celery, leek, shallots and garlic, 1 bay leaf, 1 sprig of thyme, 1 sprig of rosemary and a pinch of black peppercorns

For the potato rosti:

2 baking potatoes or 8 waxy potatoes, peeled

1 banana shallot

A pinch of caraway seeds

28g duck fat

For the creamed cabbage:

250g spring cabbage

1 banana shallot

100g smoked bacon lardons

50g pine kernels

100ml double cream

Nutmeg, salt and pepper

For the optional crust:

Brioche crumbs, garlic, parsley, Parmesan

Method

For the confit duck

To prepare the duck, trim the duck legs, removing any excess fat and sinews, then rub the legs in the herb salt rub and refrigerate overnight.

Brush the salt mix off the legs removing most of it. Heat a shallow non-stick pan and seal the duck legs all over, around 1 minute each side, remove them from the pan and sweat off the mirepoix. Place the vegetables in an ovenproof dish, top with the duck legs and barely cover with the duck fat. Place in a preheated oven at around 150-160°c and cook for 2½ to 3 hours. When thoroughly cooked remove from the oven and leave to cool, then refrigerate.

For the potato rosti

Grate the potato, mix with sliced shallots and some caraway seeds, season and leave for an hour. Then take the potato mix and squeeze out any excess water. In a non-stick frying pan heat some duck fat, place a round cutter in the cnetre and fill it with rosti mix. Cook then turn over. If you prefer to place in the oven to cook this should take 15 to 20 minutes according to the method you choose and temperature. Keep warm till you are ready to serve.

For the creamed cabbage

Slice the cabbage and shallots into pieces roughly the same as matchsticks in size. In a non-stick frying pan, sweat off some bacon lardons and the sliced shallots, add the cabbage and gently sweat for a few minutes without colouring, then add cream and pine kernels, reduce till you have the desired consistency and season to taste with nutmeg, salt and pepper.

To serve

Reheat the confit duck leg skin side down until it reaches a core temperature of minimum 82°c. The duck skin should be crispy and the meat should be falling off the bone. Present on a warm plate with some creamed cabbage and the potato rosti.

Top of their GAME

A new arrival in the West End, Leiper's Attic has found its place in the local food scene with a creative approach to showcasing Scotland's larder and warm hospitality at the top of a familiar building.

The imposing red sandstone terraces, meandering lanes and pockets of parkland give the West End a distinctive sense of place within Glasgow. It's here, on Hyndland Street, that Leiper's Attic has been carving out a reputation for serving a fine selection of wild game, wild fish and in-house dry aged beef dishes, within the confines of a much-loved local landmark.

You'll find them at the top of a winding staircase in Cottiers, the popular theatre and wedding venue created when the Four Acres Charitable Trust set about preserving the Dowanhill Church more than 20 years ago. The imposing building was named after William Leiper, the celebrated architect who created it in 1865, in conjunction with Daniel Cottier.

Leiper's Attic has a distinctive dining room, formal but with a hint of fun. It's the kind of place where you can relax and enjoy your conversation between dishes. The restaurant embraces the traditional setting but with some modern flourishes. There's space for around 60 people. Note the dry-aging cabinets for meat near the kitchen, which give you a clear view of what to expect on the menu. The bar stocks a wide selection of gins, if you care for a drink before dinner.

There is a modern French brasserie influence on the cooking style. The kitchen see it as their mission to showcase Scotland's larder. All the beef served from the grill is aged in house for 28 days. They pay special attention to provenance, working with local suppliers to source prize cuts from herds in Perthshire or Renfrewshire. Then there is the game, with Leiper's Attic striving to serve ingredients like wild duck or pheasant, which is included in their recipe for this book. You can also expect colourful vegetables with roast cauliflower, crispy kale and salsa verde regularly featuring on popular dishes. Save room for dessert, with exquisite creations like apple millefeuille with marmalade ice cream and toasted hazelnuts.

The menu changes with the seasons, allowing the best available ingredients to shine through a selection of beautifully presented dishes. The cooking is ambitious without being fussy. Staff glide between tables and have warm interactions with diners. At just over a year old, Leiper's Attic is a relative newcomer to the local community but this charming restaurant already stands out from the crowd.

Leiper's Attic

Leiper's Attic
PHEASANT BREAST, APPLE AND CIDER JUS, SHALLOT AND KALE

Leiper's Attic at Cottiers specialise in wild game and fish dishes. They strive to use the best produce Scotland has to offer and champion pheasant, a versatile ingredient that is easy to prepare and cook at home.

Preparation time: 15 minutes | Cooking time: 30 minutes | Serves: 4

Ingredients

For the shallot purée and shallots:

50g butter

500g banana shallots

50ml double cream

2 sprigs of thyme

For the apple and cider jus:

1 apple

100ml cider

50ml chicken stock

50ml double cream

1 tbsp wholegrain mustard

1 tsp lemon juice

1 tbsp chopped chives

For the pheasant:

4 pheasant breasts, seasoned

50ml chicken stock

50g butter

To serve:

100g kale

Method

For the shallot purée and shallots

Melt the butter in a pan, add 300g of chopped shallots, lower the heat and slowly caramelise. Add the double cream and bring to the boil. Remove from the heat, blend and pass through a sieve.

Halve the remaining shallots, leaving the skin on, then place in a hot pan with some oil and a sprig of thyme. Place into a 180°c oven for 3 to 4 minutes until soft, remove from the oven and allow to cool slightly before peeling.

For the apple and cider jus

Scoop out balls of apple with a parisienne scoop then add to a hot pan with a small amount of oil and lightly colour. Add the cider and reduce by half, then add the chicken stock and reduce by half again. Add the cream and reduce until the jus is the correct consistency. Finish the sauce with the mustard, lemon juice and chopped chives.

For the pheasant

Heat a little oil in a frying pan. Place the seasoned pheasant breasts skin side down and fry for 2 to 3 minutes on each side. Add the chicken stock and butter to the pan and baste the pheasant until glazed. Remove the pheasant and allow to rest for 2 to 3 minutes before serving. Keep the pan warm to heat the shallots and kale through.

To serve

Thinly slice the kale and cook in boiling salted water for 30 seconds, drop into iced water, then reheat in the pan used for the pheasant. Assemble the ingredients on plates and serve.

Fine dining
ON THE LOCH

Choose the country life, a short journey from Glasgow, and relax in plush surroundings as you discover the best of Scottish hospitality at Loch Lomond.

The Lodge on Loch Lomond Hotel sits on the beachfront at the village of Luss, where you can enjoy magnificent panoramic views over Scotland's favourite loch. It's popular for weekends away, conferences and wedding receptions. You can get there in about 30 minutes when driving from Glasgow.

Swap the buzz of the city for this tranquil setting of immaculate landscapes and outstanding produce. The charming staff at Colquhoun's Restaurant and Lounge will find you a comfy seat to enjoy your meal or, when the weather allows, the outdoor terrace is a sun trap right on the water. You will feel like you are at the heart of the loch.

The menu has some noticeable international flourishes but ultimately serves as a showcase for the best of Scotland. The hotel's Johnny Aitken explains: "We try to deliver unbeatable hospitality. Part of that is service and guest experience. The setting is another element. Then there's the food itself.

"We make our own haggis, fish and shellfish comes direct from Loch Fyne and we forage for a lot of the ingredients.

"This morning, in fact, on the way to work, I got about four hen-of-the-wood mushrooms. We bring wild food into the restaurant."

There are classic dishes that remain on the menu but the food tends to be seasonal, governed by the availability of ingredients like Shetland mussels, duck eggs from local farmers or west coast smoked salmon. As a busy wedding venue the team are used to tailoring menus to individual tastes.

The cooking is rooted in the traditional while taking account of modern tastes and trends. The kitchen aims to impress across every element of the meal. Colquhoun's Restaurant holds an AA 2 Rosettes award for Culinary Excellence.

When you visit, expect crisp white table cloths, impressive backdrop, attentive staff and the highest standard of food and wine. The 4-star Lodge on Loch Lomond is a regional treasure.

THE LODGE GIN BAR
56° 6' 17.64" N 4° 38' 21.12" W

Lodge on Loch Lomond
VENISON

A taste of wild Scottish produce and a hearty country dish, this venison recipe brings four star fine dining to your own kitchen.

Preparation time: 30 minutes | Cooking time: 2 hours | Serves: 4

Ingredients

For the venison:

4 x 180g pieces of venison loin

250g dry breadcrumbs

60g parsley, chopped

10g thyme, chopped

10g rosemary, chopped

15ml oil

10g butter

1-2 tbsp mustard

For the cherry tomatoes:

8 cherry tomatoes

½ tbsp mixed chopped herbs

Pinch of salt and sugar

For the poached pears:

1 tin baby pears (or 1 pear, peeled and quartered)

200ml red wine

50g sugar

1 sprig of thyme

1 sprig of rosemary

½ cinnamon stick

2 cloves

1 star anise

For the parsnip purée:

2 large parsnips (1 extra for crisps)

100ml milk

Double cream

20ml honey

Salt

For the girolles:

60-80g girolle mushrooms

20g butter, and oil for frying

For the sauce:

1kg venison bones (beef bones or veal bones will work)

75g carrots, 75g leeks, 75g white onion

5g tomato purée

100ml red wine, 50ml Port

600ml chicken stock

400ml beef stock

100g bitter dark chocolate

Method

For the venison

Preheat the oven to 180°c. Season the venison well with salt before searing in a hot pan. Place in the oven for 4-6 minutes (times will vary for how well done you prefer the meat). Allow to rest for 10 minutes. Blend all the other ingredients for the herb crust together and spread onto the venison, using a little mustard to help it stick.

For the cherry tomatoes

Preheat the oven to 80°c. Blanch the tomatoes in boiling water for 5 seconds, then cool in iced water. Peel off the skin then cover with a drizzle of oil and the chopped herbs, salt and sugar.

For the poached pears

Place the pears in a small pot, cover with the red wine, add all the other ingredients, bring to the boil, then simmer gently until the pears are soft.

For the parsnip purée

Peel the parsnips, put them in a small pan, add the milk and enough cream to completely cover the parsnips. Cook on a slow heat until they have completely broken down and the cream looks like it has started to split. Now blend and add honey and salt to your liking.

For the crisps and mushrooms

Peel the parsnip and discard the skin, then keep peeling to get large ribbons. Cut these into triangles and fry in oil until golden brown. To cook the mushrooms, gently heat up a pan with a little oil and fry the mushrooms. Add butter and season with salt then make sure the crisps and mushrooms are well drained on a kitchen towel before serving.

For the sauce

Heat the oven to 180°c. Roast the bones for 30-40 minutes or until golden brown. Roast the vegetables and tomato purée in a large pot, then add the roasted bones. Now add the alcohol and stocks, simmer for 45-60 minutes, pass through a fine sieve and reduce till the sauce coats the back of a spoon. Now take off the heat and, while warm, whisk in pieces of dark chocolate to get a smooth silky finish before serving.

To serve

Place a venison loin just off centre on the plate before surrounding randomly with the cherry tomatoes, slices of poached pear and large dots of parsnip purée. Top with the parsnip crisps and mushrooms before drizzling the sauce around the plate.

Eastern PROMISE

Passionate about Asian cuisine and winner of multiple awards, Jimmy Lee brings style and fresh flavours to oriental cooking in Glasgow.

Jimmy Lee is the owner and head chef of Glasgow's leading Cantonese restaurant, Lychee Oriental, on Mitchell Street. His charm, infectious smile and enthusiasm for Asian food has led to a clutch of award wins, including Scottish Personality Chef of the Year at the 2018 Food & Drink Awards and Best Asian Restaurant in Scotland at the Entertainment Awards.

Jimmy also has a burgeoning media career, appearing on the BBC's Great British Menu, Channel 4's My Kitchen Rules and presenting cookery segments for STV. He started work in his dad's takeaway when he was 16 years old and has seldom been far from a kitchen since.

At Lychee Oriental, the team pride themselves on using traditional Chinese cooking techniques and natural, fresh ingredients to create a superior dining experience. The chefs love to cook with Scottish ingredients, sourcing game or fish to incorporate them into dishes. They'll wok fry Scottish mussels with chillies and black beans or steam scallops with garlic, ginger and spring onion for impressive results.

Lychee Oriental is a stylish, contemporary space which attracts a fashionable city centre crowd. The food has Hong Kong influences with excursions to neighbouring cuisines: Vietnamese king prawn rolls, Thai red curry, Japanese chicken katsu, Singapore noodles and plenty more.

Situated within a short stroll of Buchanan Street and close to Central Station, Lychee Oriental is the ideal venue for a leisurely lunch, fun-filled dinner with friends or special occasion.

Lychee Oriental
CHAR SIU ROAST PORK

Jimmy Lee prides himself on championing traditional Chinese cooking techniques and natural, fresh ingredients. Char Siu is a popular way to season and prepare pork in Cantonese cuisine.

Preparation time: 4 hours | Cooking time: 50 minutes | Serves: 3-4

Ingredients

2 tbsp hoi sin sauce

1 tbsp oyster sauce

1 cube of red fermented beancurd (optional)

100ml red wine

½ tsp Chinese five spice

2 tbsp dark soy sauce

2 tbsp light soy sauce

3 cloves of garlic, crushed

400g pork tenderloin

1 tbsp honey

Method

Mix all the ingredients except for the pork and honey together in a small bowl. Coat the tenderloin in the marinade and then leave to marinate in the fridge for 4 hours.

Heat the oven to 180°c and roast the meat on a tray for 20 minutes. Turn over and then roast for another 15 minutes. Turn the temperature up to 220°c while you glaze the pork with honey, then roast for another 5 minutes. Take the tenderloin out of the oven and leave to rest for 10 minutes. Slice and serve.

Happy EATING
HOPE YOU ENJOY
COOKING THE
RECIPES

Hooked on
HOPE STREET

Award-winning Scottish seafood restaurant Mussel Inn was founded 20 years ago by a mussel farmer and a scallop farmer who decided to get together to buck the trend of Scottish shellfish being immediately exported to the continent by making it available in Scotland in their own restaurant.

The first Mussel Inn opened in Edinburgh in 1998. A second restaurant opened in Glasgow in 2001. Known for its passion for delicious locally sourced fresh seafood, meat dishes and vegetarian dishes, providing excellent value for money and a quick and friendly service, Mussel Inn is headed up by Swede Janne Johansson with his sons Matt and Kristian, whose direct close contact with their shellfish farmer associates ensures they receive the best quality produce available at any given time.

As a young man, Janne was a gold medal pastry chef for a world cruise company, sailing around the world before travelling around South America. He then took to the skies to oversee the provision of airline catering services throughout the Middle East, working in Bangladesh, Greece, Abu Dhabi, Dubai, Oman and Iraq, where he was held hostage during the first Gulf War.

Janne then relocated to China to set up and run a restaurant, prior to moving to Moscow before returning to Sweden when he read in a newspaper of a restaurant in Fort William looking for a pastry chef, where he spent six months before relocating to Oban, where he met his wife.

When Mussel Inn first opened, not many diners ate mussels and it played a role in helping introduce shellfish into the mainstream Scottish diet. Its mussels are grown on ropes in sea lochs on the West of Scotland and the Shetland Isles. They feed naturally in the plankton-rich waters. Sustainability and care for the environment are of utmost importance to its growers.

Its sustainably cultivated oysters, nurtured in the cold, clear sea lochs of the west coast, grow more slowly than those from warmer waters, providing a richness and depth of taste that is unique.

Yet, despite its name, the restaurant means much more to diners than just mussels. While mussels remain a staple of its menu, it now offers a broader selection of fresh Scottish seafood dishes than ever before, including: grilled queenies; piri piri tiger prawns; crab salad; queen scallops; sea bass; tiger prawns; pan-fried king scallops; char-grilled scallops; shellfish pasta and chilled or grilled oysters.

Such is its passion for seafood that Mussel Inn raises funds for Fishermen's Mission, the Royal National Mission to Deep Sea Fishermen.

Mussel Inn
MINI SEAFOOD PLATTER

Prepared with a rich shellfish sauce, topped with crème fraîche, this perennially popular dish offers a fantastic variety of tastes, textures and aromas from the sea to make your tastebuds tingle.

Preparation time: 10 minutes | Cooking time: 20 minutes | Serves: 4

Ingredients

For the shellfish sauce:

60g butter

30g shallots, finely diced

2 cloves of garlic, pressed

150ml dry white wine

350ml cooking juices from shellfish, such as mussels, clams and prawn shells

50g tomato purée

250ml double cream

5g chopped tarragon

1 pinch of saffron threads

For the sea bass:

2 sea bass fillets, cut in half

Olive oil

Salt and freshly ground pepper

For the mussels:

150ml dry white wine

400g mussels, scrubbed and beards removed

300ml fish stock

12 tiger prawns, peeled and deveined

160g cod or coley fillet, cubed

For the scallops:

1 tbsp olive oil

4 king scallops

12 queen scallops in the shell

To serve:

Crème fraîche

Half a lemon, cut into four wedges

Method

For the shellfish sauce

In a saucepan, melt the butter over a low heat. Add the shallots and garlic, then sweat for 1 to 2 minutes until soft. Pour in the wine and reduce by half, then pour in the shellfish juices. Bring up to the boil, then lower the heat and cook gently, reducing the stock by two thirds. Add the tomato purée, double cream, chopped tarragon and saffron threads.

Let the sauce bubble away gently for 10 minutes or until it will lightly cover the back of a spoon. Then strain through a sieve and season to taste. Set the sauce aside ready for the next stage.

For the sea bass

Place the four half sea bass fillets on a large baking tray, skin side up, drizzle with some olive oil and season. Put them under the grill for 2 to 3 minutes. In the meantime place a large saucepan on a high heat.

For the mussels

Add the dry white wine to the heated pan and bring it to the boil, then add the mussels and fish stock and cover, continuing to boil. After a couple of minutes, when the mussels start to open, add the tiger prawns, cubed coley fillets and the shellfish sauce. Remove the sea bass fillets from the grill (they should have started to lightly colour) and set aside. Again bring to the boil and simmer for 3 to 4 minutes or until the sauce is smooth and glossy.

For the scallops

In a large frying pan heat some olive oil and the king scallops each side for 1 minute. Then add those and the queen scallops to the baking tray with the sea bass and place under the grill for a further 3 to 4 minutes.

The queen scallops should turn opaque and the sea bass skin should be crisp. Ladle the mussels, prawns, coley and sauce evenly into four warm bowls. Then arrange three queen scallops, one king scallop and one half sea bass fillet on top of each bowl. Finish with a spoonful of crème fraîche and a lemon wedge.

Mussel Inn
PEPPERED MACKEREL PÂTÉ

A simple preparation of strong, complementary flavours.
Try the Mussel Inn's mackerel pâté recipe for yourself.

Preparation time: 24 hours | Cooking time: 15 minutes | Serves: 4

Ingredients

For the pickled radish:

240g radishes, quartered

120ml white wine vinegar

600ml water

½ tbsp mustard seeds

1 bay leaf

10g sugar

10g salt

For the pickled cucumber:

400ml water

½ tbsp mustard seeds

1 bay leaf

1 sprig of fresh tarragon

30ml white wine vinegar

2 whole black peppercorns

1 cucumber

For the pâté:

250g peppered mackerel fillets

60g crème fraîche

25ml lemon juice

Pinch of paprika

For the horseradish purée:

150g horseradish

350ml water

150ml double cream

Pinch of paprika

Method

For the pickled radish

Place all the ingredients apart from the radishes into a pot and bring to the boil. Reduce the heat and simmer for 5 minutes. While the liquid is simmering place the radishes into a suitable lidded container. Pour the warm infused liquid over the radish and close the container. Once cool place into the fridge and leave for at least 24 hours.

For the pickled cucumber

Place all the ingredients into a pot apart from the cucumber and bring to the boil. Then reduce the heat and simmer for 5 minutes to fully infuse.

Remove from the heat and pour into a suitable container to cool. While the liquid is cooling peel the cucumber into ribbons (discard the leftover seeds). Add the cucumber ribbons to the cold infused liquid, seal the container and refrigerate for 24 hours until needed.

For the pâté

Remove the skin from the fillets and break lengthways. Using your hands slowly break up each half into a bowl (taking care to remove any bones). Add the crème fraîche, lemon juice and paprika to the mackerel pieces. Then mix everything together with a fork making sure to break up any large pieces of mackerel, season to taste and refrigerate.

For the horseradish purée

Peel the horseradish and cut into small cubes. Place the cubes into a pot, cover with the water and bring to the boil. Once the horseradish is soft enough to mash with a fork, strain and reserve the water. Add the cooked horseradish, double cream, paprika and a splash of the reserved water to a blender. Blend until you have a smooth consistency (use more of the reserved water if required). Season to taste and refrigerate.

To serve

Dot the horseradish purée around each plate (four to five spots will do). Then place the pickled radish on top of the purée. Quenelle the mackerel pâté and place two quenelles on each plate. Add some of the pickled cucumber ribbons to finish the dish. Serve with toasted or charred sourdough bread.

Small room
BIG FLAVOURS

Small but perfectly formed, Nanika is chef Justin Valmassoi's take on interesting, unusual and exciting Asian food designed to challenge and delight.

Justin Valmassoi "bounced all over the place" – Detroit, Grand Rapids, Philadelphia, Chicago, Seattle – before landing in Glasgow five years ago. He kickstarted the city's fancy brunch scene with his eggs Benedict-less restaurant Something in 2015. Two years later he took over a kitchen in Shawlands and added a very popular evening concept built around Southeast Asian fare. After leaving Shawlands, he was offered a shoebox-sized space on Victoria Road and Nanika was born.

"I dated a Vietnamese girl for two years, and her family basically force-fed me all kinds of food that I had never remotely experienced before. That was so long ago now, probably the early 2000s, but that's what I tend to make if I'm cooking for myself or my friends. Those are the flavours that I gravitate towards. Vietnamese, Thai, Korean, Taiwanese. People think this is a Japanese restaurant because there is katsu curry on the menu, but it's not," Justin says.

Nanika is small. There's space for Justin in the kitchen, a server and 13 customers (18 with weather permitting). On the menu, you'll find 25-30 items with rotating specials. The equipment and logistics of the kitchen dictate what he can make. "We can't do anything that requires an open flame, basically, so we've got noodle dishes, steamed buns, interesting things on rice, etc. I don't adhere to any particular regional cuisine or plan."

It's an American approach to cooking, mixing techniques from various regions with flavours from others. Mexican elote is given a shichimi-spiked Japanese twist, for instance. People can see Justin working hard in the kitchen on their meal and he often pops out for direct feedback and a chat. To keep things interesting, he hits up the Asian markets in the north of the city looking for "weird pickles, jars of unrecognisable vegetables, and unusual food packs. If I can't read the label, I'm buying it and I figure out what to do with it later."

Go for spicy noodle bowls, Saigon salad, crispy fried tofu, jackfruit curry, chicken katsu, salmon ponzu bowls or the house kimchi. Dishes are colourful and creative. Bring your own bottle with a £2.50 corkage charge per person. Or simply "come sit very close to someone you don't know" as Nanika's motto reads, drink oolong tea and order delicious food that's new and challenging.

NANIKA

Nanika

南嘉家
72 VICTORIA ROAD
GLASGOW

SMALL THINGS

WAKAME SALAD	3.00 EACH
EDAMAME	
GAC CUCUMBERS	
VERMICELLI SALAD	
SAIGON SALAD	
ENOKI MUSHROOMS	
CHINESE BROTH	
KIMCHI NOODLE SALAD	

TODAY'S BUNS:
PORK BELLY
FRIED CHICKEN
PRAWN TEMPURA
FRIED TOFU   3.50 EACH

NOT SO SMALL THINGS

CHICKEN KATSU
SICHUAN NOODLES
SALT & CHILLI TOFU
SPICY SOUP NOODLES
JACKFRUIT CURRY
SALMON PONZU BOWL
SESAME NOODLES
THAI PORK BELLY
S&C AUBERGINES   4.00 EACH

EXTRAS

TOM YUM FRIES
S&C AUBERGINES
TOGARASHI SPROUTS
HOUSE KIMCHI & RICE
MAPO TOFU   3.75
WHITE RICE 1.00

CANS OF SODA 1.50
OOLONG TEA 1.50
DOUBLE DUTCH 2.00
B.Y.O.B
2.00 CORKAGE
(PER PERSON)

07393-710676
INSTAGRAM @NANIKA_GLASGOW

Nanika
WUHAN SESAME NOODLES

Chef Justin Valmossoi says "this dish combines all of my favourite things: spice, pickled vegetables, leftovers from other cooking jobs, and a whole lot of squeezy bottles. I've adapted it for home cooks who might not have as many squeezy bottles (and also vegans)."

Preparation time: 30 minutes | Cooking time: 10 minutes | Serves: 4

Ingredients

4 portions of fresh alkaline noodles*

Drizzle of toasted sesame oil

For the sauce:

250ml black sesame paste or tahini

15ml chianking vinegar

15ml dark soy sauce

15ml light soy sauce

1 tsp Chinese five spice

2 tbsp sugar

To serve:

200ml braising liquid**

4 tbsp light soy sauce

4 tbsp toasted sesame oil

To garnish:

Spring onions

Peanuts (optional)

Chiu Chow chilli oil (or equivalent)

Preserved vegetables***

Method

For the sauce

Combine the sesame paste or tahini with the chianking vinegar, soy sauces, five spice and sugar. Thin the sauce out with water. You can whisk it or use a food processor, as long as the end result is a slightly thick (but still pourable) and very tasty homogenous sauce with no grainy or streaky bits.

To serve

Coat each serving bowl with a layer of the sesame sauce using a silicone spatula, or just swirl the bowl with a big dollop of sauce until the inside is covered. Reheat a portion of noodles in boiling water until piping hot, drain thoroughly and add to a mixing bowl. Add 50ml of braising liquid, one tablespoon of soy sauce, and one tablespoon of sesame oil. Stir to combine. Add to the pre-sauced bowl and repeat with the remaining three portions. Slice the spring onions and bash up some roasted peanuts if using. Top each bowl with more sesame sauce, as much chilli oil as you like, a healthy sprinkle of preserved vegetables, and then garnish with spring onions and peanuts.

To eat

Stir the living hell out of the noodles to incorporate all the toppings and coat with the sesame sauce. Shovel them into your mouth and enjoy.

*Access to fresh alkaline noodles in Glasgow is relatively nonexistent, so just use a good quality egg noodle. Dried is fine. In fact, you can use spaghetti if you're stuck. Just cook, cool, and drain them, and coat with sesame oil. Reserve until needed.

**I use the braising liquid from our pork shoulder as the stock in this dish, but I doubt the average home cook is making 10kg of pork shoulder regularly, plus it's not vegetarian if you do, so we suggest taking 500ml of vegetable stock and adding ginger, star anise, black cardamom, Sichuan peppercorns, dried chillies, bay leaves, brown sugar, a dash of Shaoxing cooking wine (or dry sherry) and some soy sauce. Reduce it by at least half until you have a freakishly flavourful liquid that is almost too strong to sip on its own. Strain the solids and reserve the hot liquid.

***Preserved radish is available in small packets from almost any Chinese market in town, or you can buy tins of preserved vegetable from the same. Salt and spiciness vary but we opt for the saltier kind, so that once diced it's reminiscent of capers. It's your call, though. You're eating this. Just finely dice so it spreads evenly throughout the noodles when you stir them.

Loch Fyne DINING

The Oystercatcher is a relaxed, contemporary pub and restaurant on the East banks of Loch Fyne. It specialises in local seafood and stocks a large range of Scottish craft beers and small batch gin.

Today there's a quiet sense of calm around The Oystercatcher. Husband and wife team Dave Wall and Chloe Stapleton have just finished serving lunches filled with Ballimore oysters, Evanachan cheese – both from within a mile – local mussels, crab and meat from Argyll farms. They are eight miles outside of Tighnabruaich, down three single track roads in the countryside, but the food and the views bring a crowd.

"We're on a private estate. It's very pretty. Lots of hills and lochs to see. In the sunshine it's spectacular," Dave says. Fish and seafood are the main draws. "We've turned the place into a seafood destination for the area. We get the best of the local mussels and crab. We have a guy who comes in with scallops, fresh off the pontoon, still alive. They are really lovely. In the season when the boats are out, folk will drop off mackerel if they've caught too much and exchange it for beer."

"Apart from our regular suppliers, we've a nice relationship with a lot of people locally. It's a proper luxury to have ingredients dropped off straight out the loch."

Fish and chips is always on the menu but the rest of the dishes tend to follow the seasons. It's Scottish bar food cooked to the highest possible standard. "We've got a really nice local pork supplier so we do free-range pork. And we've got lamb off the hills or hog or sometimes even mutton or salt-marsh lamb. Sometimes we bring in highland beef. I try to get the best ingredients I can. It helps that everything is basically on our doorstep."

Dave is from Sutherland and Chloe is Australian. They met on the Isle of Iona. They lived in Australia for a while but dreamed of opening their own place, here on the west coast. Dave and the other chef, Simon, have both travelled and incorporate a lot of Asian influences to the menu; right now they are adding curry dishes. It's a short menu but covers a lot of ground. "We take inspiration from everywhere. We'll keep changing the dishes and talking to customers about what they like," Dave explains.

The Oystercatcher has won high praise and the couple are delighted with what they've created. "It's a stunning part of the country. Just a beautiful place to live. We arrived on a sunny day in September and we've never looked back. We've great staff and neighbours. Also, sometimes, if we can get out of work early, we can make it to Glasgow for a pizza and pint in the West End. It's the best of both worlds."

The Oystercatcher
WHOLE CHILLI CRAB

A recipe that showcases how The Oystercatcher, on the east banks of Loch Fyne, transforms local seafood from the Cowal Peninsula with creative preparation and combinations of fresh flavours.

Preparation time: 15 minutes | Cooking time: 10 minutes | Serves: 1-2

Ingredients

For the paste:

6 red chillies

4 cloves of garlic

A small bunch of coriander

50g root ginger

Stick of lemongrass

1 lime, zest and juice

1 tbsp fish sauce

Large pinch of salt

Large pinch of black pepper

Large pinch of brown sugar

100ml dry white wine

For the crab:

1 cooked Tarbert landed whole brown crab with claws cracked and dead man's fingers removed

50g butter

100ml white wine

100ml water

100ml chilli garlic paste (above)

For the garnish:

Handful of coriander leaves

2 spring onions, chopped

Handful of basil leaves

2 chillies, finely sliced

2cm fresh ginger, finely sliced

Method

Place all the paste ingredients in a blender and blend until a paste is formed.

To cook, take a spoon and remove all the brown meat from the crab head, and then place crab meat and all the other ingredients in a heavy-based saucepan with the lid on, on a high heat.

Cook for 5 minutes and then another 2 minutes with the lid off to evaporate the alcohol. Add more water if necessary to make sure the pan doesn't boil dry. Decant the crab and broth into a bowl and garnish.

Eat with thick bread and a chilli, mint and peanut salad. Drink the leftover wine.

Everything it's quacked UP TO BE

The best Scottish produce combined with confident cooking to elevate each ingredient makes Partick Duck Club an irresistible eatery.

Partick Duck Club is exactly the type of comfortable and accomplished restaurant everyone would like to have at the end of their street. Expect a stylish, compact dining room and confident cooking. The tartan clad booths are inviting and the small bar near the kitchen is a good spot to linger awhile. The venture's straightforward approach to creating dishes from excellent Scottish produce is the star attraction, though. Their duck fat fries, all loaded up with various toppings like tobacco onions, aioli and chives or Black Bomber cheese and hollandaise, are reason enough to pay a visit but there's plenty on the menu to entice.

Owners Ross McDonald and Greig Hutcheson have worked together for the past 17 years, including time with restaurateurs Gordon Yuill and Brian Maule, and at One Devonshire Gardens, Cameron House, then Cafezique before setting out on their own early 2017 in their first solo venture. The focus is on quality comfort food and Partick Duck Club is already a neighbourhood favourite, a two minute walk from Byres Road, on a residential corner on Hyndland Street.

A bit about the name: there was a tavern that stood on Old Dumbarton Road, a favourite of a group of Glasgow merchants and professors. In 1810 they formed the Duck Club of Partick and would dine each Saturday on local roast duck from the River Kelvin, served with sage and onion with green peas, and washed down with pints of ale. Not a bad way to spend the weekend.

Duck does feature prominently on the menu here but doesn't dominate. It's the meticulous attention to ingredients and flavour combinations that elevates simple starters like torched Highland brie with crisp gem lettuce and cress on toasted sourdough with truffle honey. Or salt-baked beetroot with goat's cheese cream and toasted hazelnuts.

Quality comfort food continues through the main courses with old favourites like chicken Kiev and shepherd's pie done very well and with their own modern take, alongside interesting vegetarian dishes.

Open and serving all day from 8am, seven days a week – one of the few places in the city that does so – Partick Duck Club has become known for its brunch menu with dishes like shakshuka baked eggs, duck leg and 'nduja hash and the innovative, rich combination of 24-hour beef short rib and duck eggs Benedict.

Partick Duck Club

DUCK LEG, CRISPY DUCK EGG, DUCK FAT FRIES, SPICED AND SMOKED PINEAPPLE CHUTNEY

A declaration of intent, this was the first dish to be served when neighbourhood hangout Partick Duck Club welcomed their first customers two years ago. It remains their biggest seller. Now you can try this popular recipe in your own kitchen.

Preparation time: 30 minutes | Cooking time: 12 hours | Serves: 2

Ingredients

2 plump duck legs

For the crispy eggs:

2 free-range duck eggs

50g plain flour

1 free-range egg, whisked

50g panko breadcrumbs, finely blitzed

For the chutney:

200g vegetable oil

3 shallots, finely diced

1 pineapple, peeled and cored

3 fresh chillies, finely diced

1 tsp coriander seeds

1 tsp smoked paprika

4 tbsp soft brown sugar

For the chips:

4 red skinned Rooster potatoes

200g duck fat

Method

In the restaurant we go through two main processes with the duck legs: brining for up to 6 hours in a solution of salt, sugar, star anise and herbs to get maximum flavour all the way through the meat then slow cooking the legs for 12 hours in a water bath at 75°c to ensure the meat is tender and pink all the way through. These processes are not crucial when making at home, but we recommend them. The brine can be exchanged for a simple marinade of star anise, fresh thyme, salt and mild olive oil, all placed in a bowl or sandwich bag with the duck legs and left in the fridge for anything between 2 hours and 2 days.

Preheat the oven to 170°c. Place the duck legs in a roasting tray or ovenproof pan and slowly cook for 2 to 2 and a half hours until the meat easily pulls away from the bone.

For the crispy eggs

Meanwhile, prepare the crispy eggs. Bring a saucepan of water to the boil and soft boil the duck eggs for 5 minutes. Remove and immediately place in a bowl of heavily iced water. Once completely cold, very carefully remove the shells and pat the eggs dry with kitchen paper. Prepare three bowls, one containing the flour, one containing the whisked egg and one containing the fine panko breadcrumbs. Completely coat the duck eggs in flour, then dip in egg and finally completely coat in breadcrumbs. Place in the fridge until ready to fry.

For the chutney

Heat a drizzle of vegetable oil in a non-stick pan and soften the shallots on a low heat. Roughly chop and add the pineapple with the chilli, coriander seeds, smoked paprika and sugar. Slowly bring the mixture just to the boil then turn the heat down and slowly simmer for 45 minutes until thick and sticky.

For the chips

Cut the potatoes into your preferred size of chip then run under cold water to remove excess starch. Blanch the chips in the remaining vegetable oil at 130°c until soft but without colour. Cool completely.

Bring the vegetable oil to 180°c in a large pan, and fry the coated duck eggs for 2 minutes. Transfer to the oven for a final 4 minutes. Heat the duck fat to 180°c in a large pan and fry the chips until golden.

To serve

Arrange the chips on one half of a large plate and sit the duck leg on top of the chips. Finely trim the top and bottom of the eggs then cut in half and sit side by side showing the soft yolks. Finish with a spoonful of the chutney.

Passion and GUTS

Serving up lunchtime sandwiches for the last ten years, Piece has always accentuated its big personality. Interactions with customers is as much a part of it's success as the outstanding flavour combinations.

'Live Piece Show' reads the glowing neon sign in the windows of a growing band of distinctive sandwich shops across Glasgow. Their fun and irreverent style is underpinned by a serious idea: to take a lunchtime staple – the humble sandwich – and create an icon. In Scotland, and Glasgow in particular, piece generally means sandwich, so the Glaswegian cultural and geographical description was the only choice for the name of this flourishing business.

The newest Piece on Waterloo Street joins locations on Argyle Street in Finnieston, West Regent Street, Miller Street, within The Whisky Bond collaborative workspace on Dawson Road and the Inovo building on Albion Street. Each branch draws in its own customers, but they all receive the same service. It's about making an impression, getting the food right and having fun. Founder John Moore explains that "most people would have around three sandwiches a week; we started Piece to make that into five sandwiches a week. We now have regulars in every single day and we work hard to inspire that loyalty and give them something new to try."

John and his co-founder Tom Lauckner decided to start the business because they couldn't find sandwiches and coffee in the city centre that lived up to their own expectations. "It really was that simple," John says. "Everything grew from there. We hired really good people, looked after them, taught them how to make the right sandwiches." Most recently, director Jon MacDonald came on board to help them make the right decisions.

To the whole team, a sandwich is just a sandwich but a piece is more. It's intertwined with Scotland and John's country of birth, Ireland. "This isn't gentrification; we just weaponised lunch," he says. "Our customers get this. They have an ownership and critique of every move we make that we love and fear in equal measure. We aren't for everyone but those who get us, really get us."

Piece's soups, coffee roasted in-house and delicious cakes are all worthy of a mention, but it's focus is undeniable. "We want to be known for one thing and be the best at it"… in other words, when people in Glasgow say they're going for a piece nowadays, they're heading for a very particular Piece!

PIECE WLS

BREAKFAST

SMOOTHIES ASK FOR FLAVOURS 3.50
PASTRIES 2.00
GRANOLA POTS OUT 2.50 IN 3.00
SOURDOUGH w/ AVO 3.00
+ EGG, HARISSA 3.50
SPICED ONIONS, SPINACH 3.50
HAM, EGG, SRIRACHA 4.00
SALMON, EGG, HONEY MUSTARD 4.50

piece [pee-ss]: artist

YAM, EGG & CHIPS

HUMMER-FALAFEL-

BIG YIN
RANDI
SCANDI

i'm a dirty fat boy

Piece
THE JERKOFF

A lunchtime favourite, this is Piece's only Caribbean style sandwich on their creative and quirky menu. The jerkoff. It was a joke and now it's in a cookbook.

Preparation time: 10 minutes | Cooking time: 6 hours | Makes: 4 sandwiches

Ingredients

For the marinated pulled pork:

1 joint of pork shoulder

2 peppers

1 tbsp fennel seeds

1 tbsp salt

2 tbsp oregano

3-4 cloves of garlic

1 large lemon, juiced

500ml olive oil

250ml water

For the spiced onions:

2 medium red onions

1 large lemon, juiced

1 tsp salt

1 tsp mustard seeds

1 tsp ground coriander

1 tsp ground cumin

1 tsp ground turmeric

Dash of oil

30g fresh coriander, chopped

For the cumin roasted sweet potato:

2 sweet potatoes, washed skin on

Pinch of salt

Pinch of cumin

Dash of oil

For the pineapple chutney:

1 large ripe pineapple, riper the better

1 white onion

1 large red chilli

5 cloves of garlic

100g white sugar

100ml white wine vinegar

To make the sandwich:

An authentic jerk hot sauce

Pickled chilli peppers, we use Melis authentic pickled peppers

Method

For the pork

Liberally season the pork and stick in the oven at 150°c for 6 hours (or until it falls apart). Leave to rest, then pull apart.

For the marinade

Dice the peppers and fry in a pan with a splash of oil and the fennel seeds. In a large mixing bowl add the oregano, garlic, lemon juice and salt to the oil and water. Once the peppers and fennel seeds are sweated down add to mixture and blend with a hand blender to a liquid.

For the spiced onions

Slice the onions and stick in a large bowl with the lemon juice and salt. Add all the spices and oil to a pan and fry on a medium to low heat until the seeds start popping. Add the hot mixture into the onions and then chuck in the coriander. Mix well by hand (using gloves if you have them!).

For the cumin roasted sweet potato

Thoroughly wash the sweet potatoes and then cut into roughly 3cm slices and lay on a tray. Add salt, cumin and drizzle with the oil. Roast at 180°c for 45-55 minutes until soft and starting to brown

For the pineapple chutney

Slice the onion and chilli, roughly smash the garlic and add it all to a medium pot. Once starting to brown, add the pineapple. Turn down the heat and simmer for 1 hour. Add the sugar and the white wine vinegar, simmer for 10 minutes then take off the heat. Once cooled, blend.

To make the sandwich

Assemble the pineapple chutney, pork, jerk sauce, sweet potato, spiced onions and pickled chillies between two thick slices of malted bread.

Food with STYLE

Meet the team behind some of Glasgow's most loved restaurants. Pioneers for the hospitality industry, James and Louise Rusk, explain their food philosophy and what drives their business to new culinary heights.

Scotland's leading independent hospitality group, RUSK & RUSK has opened some of Glasgow's most distinctive and talked-about dining spaces in The Butchershop Bar & Grill, Hutcheson's City Grill, The 158 Club Lounge and The Spanish Butcher, which was awarded Most Stylish Restaurant at the 2018 Scottish Style Awards.

Co-founders James and Louise Rusk have succeeded in creating venues that excite the senses both on and off the plate. Together they have a passion for design, creativity and pushing the boundaries of innovation within the industry.

Their latest concept adds a Pacific beat to the RUSK & RUSK collection with the launch of So L.A., a new restaurant, bar and event space on 43 Mitchell Street which draws culinary inspiration from the lifestyle and culture of California. James Rusk explains: "So L.A. pushes the boundaries of our current offering. Our new venue is set to be a truly one of a kind drinking and dining experience. Being authentic and bringing depth to the dining experience are part of our core values, and these are reflected in everything we do. This is an extremely exciting time for us."

While RUSK & RUSK restaurants have individual character and international influences, a commitment to a high standard of service and an enthusiasm for Scottish steak and seafood along with other outstanding produce unites the group. Sustainability and traceability is a priority at RUSK & RUSK.

James and Louise talk about the artistry of restaurants, the theatre of the dining room. In each of their restaurants they have designed the whole journey with precision. "All the elements from how you are met, to how your waiter interacts with you at the table – every aspect has been thought out, there's a process. It's a major creative industry to be in, it's not just about food, it's everything from design to the graphics, to get it right it takes the coming together of many factors to create the perfect all-round experience," James says enthusiastically.

On Glasgow, Louise said "We founded RUSK & RUSK in Glasgow because we love the city and we are committed to creating amazing spaces with global appeal. At RUSK & RUSK, we are deeply committed to bringing the best, progressive cuisine and cutting-edge spaces to Scotland – From prized Scottish cuts to Galician steak, which is just phenomenal. We're also building our flavour profiles and looking at our menus, bringing in fish and great vegetarian and vegan plates."

"It's very eclectic what we do," Louise says. "We look at different countries, different cities, things that we enjoy and different experiences and figure out how it can be used to better our guest's experiences. Places where we had a good experience. We like to take little snippets of everything and being able to bring these to Glasgow's great dining scene makes it even more exceptional."

Hutchesons City Grill

WHOLE LEMON SOLE WITH BUERRE BLANC, LEMON AND PARSLEY

A simple, classic fish dish from the grand surroundings of Huchesons City Grill that's fun to try at home.

Preparation time: 10 minutes | Cooking time: 20 minutes | Serves: 1-2

Ingredients

For the beurre blanc:

50ml white wine

20ml white wine vinegar

20g shallots, finely diced

2 sprigs thyme

5 black peppercorns

150g butter, ice cold & diced

Salt, to taste

10ml cream

Chives, chopped

For the sole:

300-350g lemon sole, trimmed

Oil, for frying

20g butter

To serve:

Hand-cut chips

Salt, to taste

½ lemon wedge

Sprig of parsley

Method

Ask your fishmonger to take the top skin off the sole and trim the sides.

For the beurre blanc

Make a reduction with the white wine, vinegar, lemon juice, shallots, thyme and peppercorns. Place into a saucepan and reduce right down until large bubbles are formed, approximately a quarter of original volume. Strain the reduction into a saucepan and add in the diced cold butter, constantly moving the pan till the butter becomes a creamy thick sauce.

Check the seasoning and add cream to balance and stop it from splitting in the heat. Finish with chopped chives.

For the sole

Cook the sole, top side down, in a medium to hot, non-stick pan with a little oil. Cook until the fish is golden brown, 4-5 minutes. Flip the fish over, reduce to a low heat and add 20g butter. Allow the butter to foam and go slightly light brown in colour and baste the fish with this. Season the fish and serve with chips, half a lemon, parsley and the beurre blanc.

The 158 Club Lounge
PARMA VIOLET

Sitting in The 158 Club Lounge, with its rich, sultry décor, soulful funky jazz music and carefree ambience, you would be forgiven for getting a little bit swept up in at all. An homage to old school Glasgow glamour, The 158 is a place for spectacular Cumbrae oysters, washed down with drinks served from their carefully curated bar. The champagne and cocktail list really takes centre stage here.

Preparation time: 5 minutes | Serves: 1

Ingredients

37½ml Violette liquer

25ml Absolut vodka

25ml lemon juice

25ml gomme syrup

Egg white

For the garnish:

Viola flowers

Method

Dry shake all ingredients in a Boston cocktail shaker. Shake all ingredients with cubed ice. Double strain ingredients with a hawthorne strainer and then pour through a tea strainer into a coupe glass. Garnish with a viola flower.

The Butchershop Bar & Grill

SOFT SHELL CRAB WITH CELERIAC MISO REMOULADE

Holder of the crown for steak in Scotland and famed for a love of meat, The Butchershop Bar & Grill applies culinary techniques to other gems on the menu including this famous appetiser.

Preparation time: 15 minutes | Cooking time: 50 minutes | Serves: 4

Ingredients

For the remoulade:

100g celeriac, julienne

Salt

Lime juice

1 Granny Smith apple, julienned

½ red chilli, julienned

40g coriander, minced

For the remoulade dressing:

5g white miso paste

20ml double cream

1g tumeric

1g Dijon mustard

1 large onion, sautéed

400g tin of sweetcorn, drained

1 red chilli, roughly chopped

For the crab:

240g plain flour

10g garlic powder

10g onion powder

4g paprika

4g cayenne pepper

5g salt

1g black pepper powder

4 jumbo soft shell crabs

100ml buttermilk

Micro coriander

Method

For the remoulade

Season julienned celeriac with salt and lime juice. Leave for 30 minutes in a colander over the sink to get rid of excess water.

Add julienned apple and chilli along with the coriander.

For the remoulade dressing

Reduce all the ingredients for the remoulade dressing in a pan by half, allow to cool.

For the crab

Mix all the dry ingredients together in a bowl. Dredge the crab through the flour mix, then into the buttermilk and lastly back into the flour mix.

Deep fry for 5 minutes at 170°c in oil.

To serve

Combine the remoulade with the dressing, split between four plates and place a crab on top of each serving.

Garnish with micro coriander.

So L.A.

CHICKPEA PANISSE, CAULIFLOWER AND ALMOND PURÉE, PUY LENTIL AND SQUASH SALAD

Fresh new flavours with a Californian spirit, from the innovative addition to Mitchell Street, the latest RUSK & RUSK culinary project.

Preparation time: 5 minutes | Cooking time: 10 minutes | Serves: 1-2

Ingredients

For the panisse:

350ml olive oil

2 litres water

450g chickpea flour

10g table salt

For the cauliflower purée:

1 cauliflower

600ml almond milk

Salt, to taste

For the squash and lentil salad:

1 butternut squash

3 large sprigs of thyme

300g Puy lentils

600ml vegetable stock

5g chopped parsley

Method

For the panisse

Bring the water and olive oil to a boil in a wide pan. Add the flour and salt. Whisk continuously for 10-15 minutes. Pour into a greased tray and set in the fridge.

When serving, cut to desired shape and pan fry until golden and crispy.

For the cauliflower purée

Peel the cauliflower and cut into small pieces. Place in a small pot with the almond milk and bring to a simmer.

Cook gently until the cauliflower is tender. Blend until smooth and season with the salt to taste.

For the squash and lentil salad

Peel the squash and cut into large pieces. Roast in the oven with a little olive oil and the thyme sprigs at 180°c until tender.

Place the lentils and stock in a saucepan and cook gently until the lentils are soft. Mix the cooked lentils and squash, season with a little salt and add the chopped parsley.

The Spanish Butcher

IBERICA DE BELLOTTA WITH MANCHEGO TRUFFLE FRIES AND MOJO VERDE SAUCE

Iberica de bellotta is the best pork in the world due to the pigs unique acorn diet.
This dish is inspired by travels in Spain and is full of rich Mediterranean flavours.
It has found itself a cult following in Glasgow, best cooked pink!

Preparation time: 20 minutes | Cooking time: 40 minutes | Serves: 4

Ingredients

For the Presa Iberica de bellota:

700g Presa Iberica de bellota (seam boned shoulder cut of acorn-fed black-hooved Iberican pigs)

15g Maldon salt

5g vegetable oil

For the manchego truffle fries:

1kg Agria potatoes

Oil for frying

100g 3-month aged manchego cheese, finely grated

20g chives, minced

5ml black truffle oil

5ml extra-virgin olive oil

Salt to taste

For the mojo verde:

100g parsley

100g coriander

20g confit garlic

10g toasted cumin seeds

150g extra-virgin olive oil

50g shallots bruniose

Salt, to taste

25yr old Pedro Ximenez vinegar, to taste

Method

For the Presa Iberica de bellota

Preheat oven to 180°c. Heat a heavy based frying pan till smoking. Oil and season the meat and not the pan. Colour on all sides till golden brown. Place in a separate tray in the oven for 12 minutes.

Remove from the oven and rest in a warm place for at least 5 minutes. Slice and serve.

For the manchego truffle fries

Peel the potatoes. Cut into 1½ by 1½cm chips. Steam or boil until softened but not falling apart. Allow to steam dry.

Throw chips in a colander to create fissures on the outsides. Cook in a deep-fat fryer at 130°c until edges take a little bit of colour and appear to be drying out. Remove from fryer and allow to cool.

Cook for a final time in fryer at 180°c till crisp and golden. Shake off excess fat and transfer to a bowl. Mix the chips with all other ingredients.

For the mojo verde

Mix the ingredients together and then season with salt and vinegar.

A twist on the CLASSIC

Sloans is steeped in history and remains a vibrant place for events, celebrations and parties, including being home to the Friday night Sloans Ceilidh.

Tucked away off Buchanan Street, Sloans, Glasgow's oldest bar and restaurant, has a very modern social life. You will regularly find local bands playing in the main bar and there is a weekly ceilidh upstairs in the Grand Ballroom, where they also host wedding receptions. Cult classic films are often screened there. While outside you can expect barbecues in good weather or drinks events in heated alcoves during winter. Sloans has a lot of history but it remains a vibrant venue for events and celebration parties.

This is also the headquarters of the Scottish Macaroni Appreciation Club, and with good reason.

The pasta aficionados meet on the last Wednesday of the month, where four delicious versions of macaroni are served before members cast their vote for their favourite mac of the night. A mystery mac is revealed on the night, which is often a wild twist on the traditional recipe.

Macaroni cheese has long been a key component of the Glasgow pub food fundamentals. In Sloans, the well-fired, deep bowls of creamy, cheesy pasta have been elevated to an art form.

Any day of the week, there are five main staple versions to choose from. You can have macaroni cheese with natural smoked haddock. There's also Ayrshire bacon and brie or a topping of jalapeño and cheddar. Parmesan and sun blushed tomatoes is an option, along with whatever the Appreciation Club have picked as macaroni of the month. If this is your favourite comfort food, you've come to the right place.

Other highlights from the bar menu include the steak and Kelburn ale pie and ever popular fish and chips. At the bar, Sloans has Scottish craft ale and canned beer, prosecco and 40 different types of gin.

If you also crave a satisfying portion of mac 'n' cheese, follow their recipe at home or join the pasta party at Sloans.

Sloans
LEGENDARY MACARONI CHEESE

A Sloans favourite for over 10 years, selling over 20,000 helpings a year, this mac 'n' cheese has its own fan club – The Scottish Macaroni Appreciation Society – who meet in the bar every month to pledge their allegiance to the cheesy dish. It's a classic, creamy, hearty dinner for all the family. Best to cook in big batches because once your friends and family see it they'll all want a plate.

Preparation time: 30 minutes | Cooking time: 30 minutes | Serves: 12-15

Ingredients

2 litres whole milk

2g ground white pepper

2g ground nutmeg

45g salt

300g butter

300g plain flour

1kg mature white cheddar, grated

200g Dijon mustard

600g Marshalls macaroni pasta

Method

In a thin-based pot, mix the milk, white pepper, nutmeg and salt and heat until warm. Then, take a separate pot and melt the butter. Once the butter has melted, fold in the plain flour and cook for 5 minutes, stirring constantly until smooth.

On a low heat, combine both the flour and milk mixtures together. Take off the heat and add the cheddar and mustard to the mixture, then fold together using a whisk or hand-held blender. Cook the pasta until al dente, drain and add the cheese sauce to the pasta.

Pour your macaroni cheese into an ovenproof dish and sprinkle with cheddar cheese and any other cooked toppings of your choice; why not try some Sloans favourites like bacon and brie or Parmesan and sun-dried tomatoes.

Heat the mac 'n' cheese in a preheated oven at 180°c for 30 minutes or until golden.

Serve with Glasgow salad: a plate of chips.

Smell the COFFEE

Awesome coffee, excellent food, friendly folk and a welcoming place to relax. Join the crowd at Spitfire Espresso.

Spitfire Espresso occupies one of the great vantage points in the Merchant City, across from the Ramshorn Theatre building and with a view of the bustling city. The team are a friendly bunch, led by husband and wife Danny and Emily Gorton. Visit for an excellent cup of coffee, served with a smile and an easy chat.

The story so far: Emily and Danny got married in 2012, then left their corporate jobs in London "to move to New Zealand for a change of lifestyle and to work out what we wanted to do with our lives," says Danny. There, Danny spent some time working in the speciality coffee industry with Flight Coffee gaining valuable insight into the 'third wave', commonly known as speciality coffee.

"All of a sudden, I fell back in love with the hospitality industry. I realised that now, with a lot more life experience under my belt, I had the tools to run a café of my own!" he says, enthusiastically. Meanwhile, Emily had a background in buying so would be prepared for running the back office side of the business.

They decided to move before embarking on this exciting new venture, considering a number of different UK locations. Attracted by news of the city's developing coffee and food scenes, the Gortons decided on Glasgow. From reliable, friendly enclaves for creative types, places to enjoy a pot of tea and slices of carrot cake while fidgeting with smartphones, meeting places for mums with ample buggy parking to quiet tables for conspiratorial chats and expansive gossip sessions, Spitfire Espresso fits into the pantheon of local independent cafés looking to do things their own way.

Danny explains the business model for Spitfire as simply "carefully sourced coffee made with care, eggs done really well, a selection of cakes and sandwiches to cover all tastes, a vegan menu and beer available on draft and by the bottle, as well as wine and spirits." Their Gunnerbean coffee is a delicious blend of Colombian and Brazilian beans, ideal for drinking as a simple espresso, or with milk in a flat white or latte. The food menu features wonderful eggs from Pennyfield farm, cooked meats from Puddledubs Farm, milk from Mossguil Farm, breads from The Gingerbread Man, fruit and vegetables from Seasonal Produce and salmon from Fish Plaice. Their commitment to local produce reflects Spitfire's community spirit, where staff and regulars are on first name terms and the friendly atmosphere is a cornerstone of the business.

Spitfire Espresso
SUPER SIMPLE SPITFIRE BROWNIES

Spitfire Espresso is a friendly, laid back, independent coffee spot in the Merchant City where they serve exceptional coffee, a satisfying all day breakfast and tasty bakes like these delicious brownies.

Preparation time: 15 minutes | Cooking time: 35-45 minutes | Makes: 18

Ingredients

350g unsalted butter

350g caster sugar

350g dark chocolate

8 eggs

Method

Preheat a fan-assisted oven to 150°c (adjust the temperature to 170°c for non fan-assisted ovens). In a bain-marie, melt the sugar and butter and stir until the mixture is smooth. Add the chocolate and stir gently until fully melted and combined with the sugar and butter mixture.

Whisk the eggs in a stand mixer at level three (medium speed) until fluffy. If you don't have a stand mixer the eggs can be whisked by hand as long as enough air is added in. Add the chocolate mixture to the eggs and continue mixing on a slow speed until well combined. Transfer the mixture to a lined and greased 15 by 30cm baking tin, about 5cm deep. Allow the lining to overhang by an extra few centimetres to make removing the brownies from the baking tin easier.

Bake for 35 to 45 minutes until the brownie has risen to about double its original height and has a gentle wobble when removed from the oven. Allow to cool completely and refrigerate before cutting. The brownie will collapse back to its original height during this time.

Cut into equal 5cm squares and serve with a strong coffee. Enjoy the brownies on their own or with Greek yoghurt, cream or ice cream on the side.

Life is SWEET

The team at Sugar Boat are bringing together local flavours in a Helensburgh kitchen that's setting new standards for hearty bistro fare while establishing its place in the West of Scotland food scene.

Restaurateur Will Smith was proud to return to Helensburgh. He had lived there while working at Cameron House before finding success in London; he started two restaurants, Wild Honey in Mayfair and Soho's Arbutus. Will has a deep affection for the Clyde Coast, as does his wife Lynn, who works as a teacher in Glasgow and is originally from Balloch. He opened his bistro, bar and wine shop here in 2017.

A conversation with head chef Scott Smith proved to be the key. Will discovered that the two shared a food philosophy, as well as a surname. He explains: "I knew Scott was from Oban, and he had worked for us for four years at two different restaurants. We met for lunch and I told him what I was thinking about doing.

"It soon became clear we had the same ethos, about hospitality, warmth and nourishment. I'm not that interested in fine dining foams, purées and gels. I want real food on a plate. We've Scott in the kitchen, cooking from the heart and giving someone a proper meal. That's been the basis of the Sugar Boat menu. I love his style of cooking." Meanwhile, restaurant manager Alastair Begg, who has been with the restaurant from the start, leads the team front of house.

The name Sugar Boat entered the vocabulary of Helensburgh residents and those along the Firth of Clyde following a fateful night in January 1974 when the MV Captayannis – a 121 metre long ship laden with a cargo of sugar – succumbed to the ravages of a winter storm. Its hull was holed by a nearby tanker's anchor chain and it rapidly keeled over on a sandbank while the captain and crew were safely rescued and taken ashore. No one ever stepped forward to move the hull, which remains visible from the shore today.

The connection to the local community is important to the bistro. Small producers often wander in with strawberries, carrots or potatoes to sell, which form the basis of a new dish. They've developed relationships with nearby farmers, bakers and fishermen. Milk is provided by an independent dairy, over the hill in the Vale of Leven and the game is from Luss estates.

Bouillabaisse has been on the menu since Sugar Boat opened. "It's been a good dish for us," Will says. "We'll always have it on the menu, and we donate 50p from each portion we sell to the local RNLI. It's an attractive dish, nourishing and very rewarding to try at home."

Sugar Boat
BOUILLABAISSE

Our version of a classic Provençal fisherman's stew, bursting with flavour and supporting a great cause.

Preparation time: 24 hours | Cooking time: 30 minutes | Serves: 6

Ingredients

For the bouillabaisse:

1.5kg red mullet, gutted but whole

1 tbsp paprika

¾ tsp cayenne pepper

Drizzle of vegetable oil

1 onion, roughly chopped

2 carrots, roughly chopped

1 bulb of fennel, roughly chopped

1 bulb of garlic, crushed

2 sticks of celery, roughly chopped

4 tomatoes, roughly chopped

150ml martini

75ml white wine

½ tsp saffron

500ml vegetable stock

1 large potato, skin on

Salt and pepper

Squeeze of lemon juice

Dash of Tabasco and Worcestershire sauce

For the garnish:

12 Jersey Royal potatoes, washed

1 bulb of fennel, cut into 6 wedges

2 leeks, greens removed and cut into 6–8cm cylinders

2 fillets of cod, scaled, pin-boned and cut into 6 portions

2 fillets of grey mullet, scaled, pin-boned and cut into 6 portions

6 fillets of red mullet, scaled and pin-boned

300g butter, cut into 6 pieces

3 sprigs of thyme

6 thin slices of sourdough bread (6mm thick), dried in the oven to a crisp

6 dollops of aioli (in the restaurant we make a saffron rouille)

Method

For the bouillabaisse

The night before, toss the fish in the paprika, cayenne and some vegetable oil. Cover and leave to marinate overnight in the fridge. The next day, roast the fish in a large pan in stages getting a good colour. Once all the fish is roasted, set aside. In the same pan sweat all the vegetables except the potato until soft, deglaze with the alcohol and then add the saffron.

Add the stock and bring to the boil, then add the fish back to the pan. Cook for 20 minutes then thinly slice the potato and add to the pot. Boil for a further 20 minutes then blitz well and pass.

Season with salt, pepper, lemon juice, Tabasco and Worcestershire sauce to taste.

Keep the soup in the fridge but bring to the boil before serving.

For the garnish

Boil the Jersey potatoes and set aside. Add the fennel and leeks to a pan and cover with the vegetable stock or water. Season well and bring to the boil, then reduce to a low simmer until the veg is soft. Set aside.

This is the tricky bit where you need to juggle cooking the fish with keeping the vegetables and soup warm at the same time… it is worth it though! Heat your largest pan, add a little oil and the colour the fish, starting with the cod skin side down. Once the cod is coloured, add the grey mullet skin side down, leaving the cod to carry on cooking in the same pan skin side down. Allow the grey mullet to crisp then add the red mullet, skin side down. Once the red mullet is crisp you should now have all three fish in the pan, skin side down. Add a large knob of butter, allow it to melt, then flip all the fish over and remove from the pan. Serve immediately.

To serve

The best way to serve bouillabaisse is in a large hot pan or terracotta dish, family style. Line the pan with the vegetables, add the fish fillets on top and garnish with a few sprigs of fresh thyme. The soup can be poured onto this base from a jug at the table and then topped with the sourdough crisps. Add dollops of aioli or rouille on the crisps for texture, and then encourage your guests to get stuck in! We recommend serving with a full-bodied white wine from the Jura region in France or a rich, nutty viognier.

Dough IDEA

Tantrum are part of a cadre of independent, distinctive food businesses in Glasgow who are leading the charge for the next wave of local flavours.

Glasgow has a sweet tooth. It's not a fad or a trend. We are committed. So when Tantrum Doughnuts, the brainchild of husband and wife team Iain and Annika Baillie began making pop-up appearances at markets, they attracted a crowd. Then came a shop on Old Dumbarton Road, which opened in December 2015 and has become a firm favourite in the neighbourhood.

For their next trick, Tantrum rolled into the city centre, with a place on Gordon Street, close to Central Station. Enter and you are greeted by a colourful, outlandish display of fun treats. Brioche doughnuts, handmade in small batches, then smothered, filled or glazed with homemade custards, fondants, purées, compotes and jams. Their selection changes when new ingredients become available from local suppliers. A current favourite is tonka bean with an orange oil infused glaze. They also serve an excellent cup of coffee.

Being a chef is all Iain has ever wanted to do. The pastry side of the work appealed to him and he had the chance to hone his technical skills when he spent two years at The Fat Duck in Bray. Returning to Glasgow, Iain sought out a job at Ox & Finch, not long after they opened, because he was impressed with their approach to cooking.

He would work there during the day before baking with Annika through the night, as they looked to establish their business. Annika has front of house hospitality experience and a keen eye for branding and marketing, one of the reasons Tantrum has such a strong presence on social media. In the early days, pictures of new doughnuts on Instagram acted as a clarion call to attract new devotees.

In January 2018, Tantrum opened a new bakery to support both shops in a converted railway arch in the contemporary SWG3 event space in Glasgow's West End. Now there's a team of pastry chefs who roll, glaze and fry through the night. "It's very hard work, and can be surprisingly overwhelming at times but at the end of the day, we get to create delicious doughnuts that make people happy and that's one of the best jobs in the world," Iain says.

The recipe they've decided to share is for traditional buttermilk doughnuts: "it's a favourite among our regulars as it's the perfect breakfast doughnut. As a non-yeasted raised doughnut, it doesn't require any proving, and is quickly fried and glazed. When they fry, the dough cracks open as the buttermilk reacts with the hot oil, and when glazed, the glaze sneaks into all those nooks and seals in the moisture. Definitely try this at home!"

Tantrum Doughnuts

OLD-FASHIONED BUTTERMILK DOUGHNUTS

Discover why Tantrum have the best doughnuts in Glasgow with this tasty recipe for a traditional sweet treat. Handmake a batch to brighten up your day.

Preparation time: 5 minutes | Cooking time: 20 minutes | Makes: 12-15

Ingredients

For the doughnut:

70g softened butter

160g caster sugar

100g egg yolks

640g strong bread flour, plus extra for dusting

5g nutmeg

10g salt

15g baking powder

290g buttermilk

Oil for frying (we use rapeseed oil)

For the glaze:

750g icing sugar

180ml milk

Natural almond extract (to taste)

Method

Combine add the butter and sugar in a stand mixer with a paddle attachment, then set the mixer to high and beat until pale and fluffy. Lower the mixer to slow, stream in the egg yolk and mix for around 2 minutes.

Stop the mixer, add 320g of the flour with the nutmeg, salt and baking powder. Mix on medium until just incorporated, then add the buttermilk and mix until it comes together, then add the rest of the flour and mix to combine.

Lightly dust your counter-top with flour. Roll out the dough with a rolling pin, to a thickness of around 6mm. Leave to rest for 2 to 3 minutes. Using a 7.5cm round cutter, dip the cutter in flour and stamp out the doughnuts. Use another 2.5cm round cutter to punch out the middles to create the non-fattening centre.

Using an electric fryer or a small pot of oil with a thermometer, heat the oil to 170°c.

Using a spatula, gently lower the doughnuts into the oil, around 2-3 at a time depending on the size of your pot. They will sink to the bottom, and then float up gently. Let them colour for around 90 seconds – the top should be cracking open and the bottom should be golden brown. Flip the doughnuts over gently with your spatula and cook for another 90 seconds. At this point they should be GBD – golden brown and delicious.

Lift out of the pot with spatula, and shake off any excess oil. Place on a kitchen towel to drain. Leave to cool slightly and repeat with all the doughnuts.

Next, it's time to glaze. Tantrum Top Tip: Glaze while the doughnuts are still warm, dip in the hot glaze cracked side down, then flip over and leave to set on a baking paper lined tray. This makes the hot glaze run into all the little nooks and crevices and set to create a delicious doughnut.

Combine the icing sugar and milk, add almond extract to taste, then whisk the mixture until completely smooth.

Give the glaze a quick blast in the microwave so the glaze is a runny consistency when you are ready to glaze your doughnuts. You can modify the flavour of the glaze to suit the tastes.

Classic COOKING

An upscale seafood restaurant with a classic approach to drinking and dining, Two Fat Ladies at The Buttery demonstrates the best standards of Glasgow hospitality.

Ryan James bought Two Fat Ladies on Dumbarton Road and then took over The Buttery twelve years ago. He also has a city centre restaurant on Blythwood Square.

The Buttery has been around for a lot longer – the building dates from 1870 – but it took a patient refurbishment and some flair in the kitchen to establish it as one of the best restaurants in the city.

On one level, it's an old-school classic, but it could also be considered something of a hipster trendsetter as, it's fair to say, Two Fat Ladies liked Finnieston before it was cool.

This is the type of place that is difficult to create, it has to evolve over time. The oak and mahogany, the plush bar and reception area, tartan carpet, stained glass. You are entering a time capsule of Glasgow hospitality that retains a sense of innovation in the kitchen.

It is a traditional dining room without being stuffy. If you took a date here, they would be impressed without being overawed. The staff glide between tables and put guests at ease. There's a buzz of easy conversation.

Two Fat Ladies at The Buttery sources ingredients from across Scotland, Ryan explains. "Most of the fish that we use is landed at Peterhead, and comes down to Glasgow. We're all fighting for the best of that produce to a certain extent, but there's certainly a plentiful supply of fish. There's also great beef, very good game as well, especially from Ayrshire."

The job of the kitchen is to make these ingredients shine and to ensure customers have a good time and leave well fed. "We let the flavours speak for themselves to a certain extent. I'm not looking to educate people or teach them new things about food, I just want to serve up the best dishes at a fair price."

Tourists who visit The Buttery are impressed with what they find. "I think people should be very proud when they talk about Scotland's larder. Sometimes we don't say that loud enough. We find visitors are totally impressed with how good the food is in Glasgow."

The recipe the restaurant has shared is a preparation of scallops, and it's one Ryan says he regularly prepares at home. "Personally, I love scallops as a main course but it's my favourite starter, followed by a beef dish and then a crème brulée. I'm a creature of habit."

Two Fat Ladies
WEST COAST SCALLOPS, GOLDEN RAISIN & SAFFRON PURÉE, SPICED CAULIFLOWER FRITTERS

We found that the fresh scallops worked well with mildly spiced, earthy tones of the cauliflower, while the raisin and saffron purée adds a touch of both sweetness and elegance.

Preparation time: 5 minutes | Cooking time: 10 minutes | Serves: 1-2

Ingredients

For the golden raisin purée:

100g golden raisins

25ml white wine

1 shallot, diced

A pinch of saffron

For the cauliflower fritters:

100g self-raising flour

100g cornflour

15g mild madras curry powder

1 cauliflower

For the scallops:

2 scallops

1 lemon, juiced

Method

For the golden raisin purée

Place all the ingredients into a saucepan and add enough water to cover the raisins. Bring to the boil and then simmer until soft. Using a hand blender, remove from the heat and purée the mixture. Pass the purée through a fine sieve, pushing it down with the back of a ladle. Season to taste and set aside.

For the cauliflower fritters

Mix all the dry ingredients together in a bowl and whisk in 250-350ml of water until you have a batter consistency. Break or cut the cauliflower into florets then cut them in half. Preheat a fryer to 165°c. Dip the florets in the batter and place one at a time into the fryer with enough room for the florets to be moved about while cooking. When lightly coloured, take the fritters out and place them on paper towels to drain.

For the scallops

Preheat the pan with a little oil in. Season the scallops and then place them into the frying pan. Check after 30 seconds to see if they've coloured nicely. When golden brown, turn over and repeat the cooking process. Finish the scallops by adding a splash of lemon juice, rolling it around the pan to deglaze and then removing the scallops from the heat.

To finish

Warm the raisin purée and create a large tear drop shape with it on the serving plate, using the back of a spoon.

Deep fry the cauliflower fritters, remove and drain when golden brown. Place the scallops and fritters on the plate with a pea shoot salad, fresh tomato and a few leaves of lemon balm to garnish.

Wild about COOKING

Justin Maule allows international cuisines to influence and inspire his recipes, which focus on the outstanding ingredients that are available in the west of Scotland.

Wild Fig is led by husband and wife team Justin and Nicola Maule. They are based in South Lanarkshire but travel widely for pop-up dining experiences, location catering for the film and TV industry or special events. You may have met them already or enjoyed their small batch, handmade products containing simple, natural ingredients.

Nicola is a strong creative influence on Wild Fig. "I was able to bring my love and experience of film and photography to the business and the brand, as well as my project management skills from my work as an art curator. Although I have never really been too far removed from hospitality, and for many years worked front of house in restaurants and bars in Glasgow city centre. This mix makes for a business where creativity is a key part but is grounded in experience of working in the industry."

Justin had a food education that started very early in his life. There was the opportunity to travel around great restaurants and hotels of Europe with his father, William Maule, who was a chef of reputed standing and served as the grounding of Justin's talents as a chef, but also an inspiration. He won Scottish Junior Cook of the Year at the age of 11, the

youngest ever to do so and his passion for food and cooking never left him, going on to work in some of the best kitchens in Scotland.

Self-development has also been a key element throughout his career; much of what Justin has learned has come from his own investigation and motivation and this continually shows in the exceptional standard of his cooking. Whether it is a humble bowl of porridge or a sumptuous banquet, Wild Fig work with abundant Scottish ingredients and look to elevate dishes with fresh ideas. They consciously embrace the diversity of sourcing globally, allowing new flavouring to influence traditional recipes.

Pooling their talents has allowed the family business to grow, with whisky pairing dinners for their corporate clients, cooking demonstrations, television appearances on STV and developing their award-winning preserve range, all part of the average eclectic week for Wild Fig.

Wild Fig
BAKED SCOTTISH HAKE, POTATO AND SAUSAGE FABADA

"This dish was served at a Wild Fig pop-up dining event and we love the flavours and simplicity of it. The traditional Spanish fabada has been made using Scottish black pudding and chorizo and the warming, earthy paprika spiked stew is the perfect foil for the meaty white flesh of the hake, which is simply baked on the fabada, producing a perfectly balanced dish."

Preparation time: 15 minutes | Cooking time: 25 minutes | Serves: 6

Ingredients

For the fabada:

Olive oil, for frying

200g waxy potatoes, peeled and sliced into discs

2 onions, peeled and sliced

4 cloves of garlic, peeled and crushed

2 tsp paprika

100g chorizo, peeled and sliced into discs

100g morcilla or black pudding

100g chopped tomatoes

2 tins butter beans, drained

100ml dry white wine

100ml water

Sea salt and pepper

For the hake:

6 x 225g portions of hake

Method

For the fabada

Heat the oil in a sauté pan or casserole dish and fry the potatoes till lightly browned. Add the onions and garlic then cook until softened. Add the paprika and fry for 2 minutes, then add the chorizo and morcilla or black pudding and fry for a further 2 minutes.

Stir in the chopped tomatoes and butter beans, add the wine and water, then season with salt and pepper. Simmer for about 3 minutes until the beans are softened and flavours combined.

For the hake

Season the hake well on both sides then place the portions on top of the fabada. Cover and simmer for 8-10 minutes, or until the hake is cooked through.

Serve with warmed crusty bread and a green salad.

Calton
CALLING

Rocking the East End with a creative approach to bar food and great taste in music, The Winged Ox at Saint Luke's is ready to entertain you.

The Winged Ox is the food and drink side of the operation at ultra-hip East End venue Saint Luke's. The stage in the converted church, with its stained-glass window backdrop, has become a cherished part of the local music scene, regularly playing host to some of the biggest touring indie acts. Meanwhile, the bar kitchen in the room next door continues to cook up its own showstopping headliners with a strong international comfort food menu that's not afraid to be ambitious.

Head chef Jay Ward is in the process of reinvigorating the established line up of popular dishes. Like the music that's played here, it's food with soul, big personality and a strong Glasgow accent.

On weekdays, The Winged Ox is where local families meet or folk pop in for an afternoon drink or an evening meal. The benches on the outside terrace are a suntrap during the summer and booths in the bar are regularly booked out at weekends so groups of pals can enjoy banter, burgers and beers.

This is a Calton venue, somewhere that's become an integral part of the community, not merely the preserve of hipster blow-ins. You'll see all the family here for dinner. Wayfarer-sunglasses-wearing-rockers of all ages are, of course, made to feel at home. It's an eclectic mix. You might even spot the occasional dog visiting The Winged Ox with its owner (If you do have a dog, there's a particular menu for canines so they can eat while you eat).

Bottles of Bourbon and gin rival the whiskies on display behind the bar. There's a rotating selection of craft beer, often from Drygate or West, so you can enjoy a good local pint. For their food philosophy, they take influences from other fashionable venues and cities. There's also a strong sense that Saint Luke's & The Winged Ox is very comfortable standing out from the crowd and serving up bar snacks less ordinary.

Saint Luke's was the result of a meticulous renovation by brothers Michael and Tony Woods, giving the east of the city another landmark venue, breathing life into a building that was hidden in plain sight, across from the entrance to the Barras and a short walk from Glasgow Green. As a bar and a restaurant, The Winged Ox provides a warm welcome and an exciting mix of food and drink seven days a week.

The Winged Ox
SHEPHERD'S PIE, CAULIFLOWER, CRISPY KALE & ROASTED ONIONS

"Being asked to create the owner's favourite meal for the menu was a great start," says Winged Ox head chef Jay Ward. "Hugely popular and an example of the dishes I like preparing, this shepherd's pie is a comfort food classic that I think you will all enjoy making in your own kitchen. Source good quality ingredients and get cooking!"

Preparation time: 30 minutes | Cooking time: 1 hour 30 minutes | Serves: 4

Ingredients

For the garnish:

Curly kale (remove leaves from the stem and tear into pieces)

Small jar of silverskin onions, drained

For the lamb filling:

500g lamb mince

1 litre chicken stock

2 small onions, finely diced

3 sticks of celery, finely diced

1 small leek, finely diced

2 small carrots, finely diced

Handful of flatleaf parsley, chopped

2 sprigs of rosemary, off the stem and chopped

2 sprigs of thyme leaves, picked from the stalk

2 cloves of garlic, chopped

For the cauliflower purée:

1 cauliflower, core removed and cut into florets

300ml double cream

300ml whole milk

For the potato topping:

6 large potatoes, peeled and quartered

2 egg yolks

100g butter, diced

60g cheddar cheese, grated

Method

For the garnish

Rub the kale all over with a little oil after washing, place on a tray and bake in a preheated oven at 150°c until crisp. Drain off the onions and fry until brown with a teaspoon of butter and tip on to paper towel.

For the lamb filling

Brown off the lamb mince in a pan, then add the rest of the vegetables and herbs. Continue to sweat for a few minutes and add half the chicken stock. simmer until almost dry and do the same with the rest of stock, season and set aside.

For the cauliflower purée

Over a medium heat cover the cauliflower with the milk and cream and simmer until the cauliflower is soft and mushy, stirring occasionally. Using a hand blender, blend until smooth and creamy.

For the potato topping

Place the potatoes in a pot with salted water and boil until ready to mash (use a potato ricer if available), drain and then return to the pot. Take out two dessert spoons of mash and add to the lamb filling for later on. While hot, fold in the egg yolks, then the diced butter until incorporated, then add the cheese and scoop into a piping bag.

To serve

Warm anything that has cooled, take two spoons of the cauliflower purée and spread in a circular motion on each plate. Mix the wee bit of mash through the lamb filling (this helps to soak up excess moisture) and divide in to four. Place a portion neatly in the centre of the cream purée and lightly flatten the top ready for the mash. Pipe the warm mash in a back and forth motion on top of the lamb and then scatter the kale and onions around to finish.

Top tips

When simmering the lamb in stock, for best result use a soup spoon to skim the fat as it rises. If you have a blowtorch, glazing the mash gives flavour and even some theatre at the table!

The DIRECTORY

These great businesses have supported the making of this book; please support and enjoy them.

158 Lounge

158 Ingram Street
Glasgow
G1 1EJ
Telephone: 0141 552 4050
Website:hutchesonsglasgow.com

Old school cocktail bar.

A'Challtainn Fish Restaurant & Bar

54 Calton Entry
Glasgow
G40 2SB
Telephone: 0141 237 9220
Website: baadglasgow.com/achalltainn

Sustainable seafood and local produce from one of the coolest places to eat in the city.

Alla Locanta

192 Pitt St
Glasgow
G2 4DY
Telephone: 0141 332 5300
Website: locanta.co.uk

Authentic family-run Italian and Mediterranean restaurant.

Baffo Pizza And Birra

1377 Argyle Street
Glasgow
G3 8AF
Telephone: 0141 583 0000
Website: baffo.co.uk

Authentic Italian pizza in a relaxed restaurant atmosphere.

Basta

561 Dumbarton Road
Glasgow
G11 6HU
Telephone: 0141 339 8698
Website: bastapizza.com

Quirky, self-professed Disco Pizza Bar mixes Italian ingredients with Partick attitude.

Battlefield Rest

55 Battlefield Road
Glasgow
G42 9GL
Telephone: 0141 636 6955
Website: battlefieldrest.co.uk

Well-loved Italian restaurant serving both traditional and experimental dishes.

Bibimbap

3 West Nile Street
Glasgow
G1 2PR
Telephone: 0141 221 6111
Website: bibimbap-glasgow.com

Fresh, authentic Korean dishes.

Billington's of Lenzie

114 Kirkintilloch Road
Kirkintilloch
Glasgow
G66 4LQ
Telephone: 0141 776 8090
Website: billingtonsoflenzie.co.uk

Fresh produce and independent flavours.

Bilson Eleven

10 Annfield Place
Dennistoun
Glasgow
G31 2XQ
Telephone: 0141 554 6259
Website: bilsoneleven.co.uk

A restaurant with a modern twist on classic flavours.

Brian Maule at Chandon d'Or

176 West Regent Street
Glasgow
G2 4RL
Telephone: 0141 248 3801
Website: brianmaule.com

A fine dining experience with award-winning dishes.

The Butchershop

1055 Sauchiehall Street
Glasgow
G3 7UD
Telephone: 0141 339 2999
Website: butchershopglasgow.com

Renowned for their succulent burgers and steaks.

Café Gandolfi

64 Albion Street
Glasgow
G1 1NY
Telephone: 0141 552 6813
Website: cafegandolfi.com

A classic restaurant using the best of specially sourced Scottish ingredients.

Catch

186 Fenwick Road
Giffnock
Glasgow
G46 6XF
Telephone: 0141 638 9169
Website: catchfishandchips.co.uk

A modern take on fish and chips.

Da Luciano Bothwell

2 Silverwells Cresent
Bothwell
Glasgow
G71 8SE
Telephone: 01698 852722
Website: dalucianobothwell.com

A signature mix of Italian and Scottish cuisine in the heart of Bothwell.

The Fish People Café

350A Scotland Street
Glasgow
G5 8QF
Telephone: 0141 429 8787
Website: thefishpeoplecafe.co.uk

Seafood, wine and hospitality on the southside.

Fruin Farm

Glen Fruin
Helensburgh
G84 9EE
Telephone: 01389 850 727
Website: fruinfarm.co.uk

A different countryside experience at Loch Lomond.

Gamba

225A West George Street
Glasgow
G2 2ND
Telephone: 0141 572 0899
Website: gamba.co.uk

Classic techniques with a modern twist.

The Gannet

1155 Argyle Street
Glasgow
G3 8TB
Telephone: 0141 204 2081
Website: thegannetgla.com

Restaurant and bar in Finnieston showcasing the best of Scottish produce.

Gather by Zique

70-72 Hyndland Street
Glasgow
G11 5PT
Telephone: 0141 339 2000
Website: www.gatherbyzique.com

Seasonal produce and fresh flavours from the people behind Cafezique.

Glasgow Gin Distillery Company

Hillington
Deanside Road
Glasgow
G52 4XB
Telephone: 0141 404 7191
Website: glasgowdistillery.com

Home of the award-winning Makar Gin, the first gin to be distilled in Glasgow.

Glasgow Life

Website: peoplemakeglasgow.com

All you need to know about visiting Glasgow.

Glasgow Taxis

Telephone: 0141 429 7070
Website: glasgowtaxis.co.uk

The largest suppliers of licensed taxis in the city.

Glasgowist

Website: hello@glasgowist.com

A website celebrating the best people and places in the city of Glasgow.

Guy Cowan

Email: spaghettib@aol.com
Telephone: 07950151703

One of the best known chefs in Glasgow.

Halloumi

161 Hope Street
Glasgow
G2 2UQ
Telephone: 0141 204 1616
Website: halloumiglasgow.co.uk

Greek restaurant serving small plates with big flavours, inspired by the beauty of Athens and the produce of the Mediterranean.

Hutchesons City Grill

158 Ingram Street
Glasgow
G1 1EJ
Telephone: 0141 552 4050
Website: hutchesonsglasgow.com

A bustling restaurant with a focus on choice Scottish beef.

La Bonne Auberge

161 West Nile Street
Glasgow
G1 2RL
Telephone: 0141 352 8310
Website: labonneauberge.co.uk

La Bonne Auberge Glasgow Theatreland is still going strong after more than 40 years.

Leiper's Attic

93-95 Hyndland Street
Glasgow
G11 5PU
Telephone: 0141 357 6825
Website: leipersattic.com

Outstanding Scottish produce cooked with flair in the West End.

Lodge on Loch Lomond

Luss
Argyll
G83 8PA
Telephone: 01436 860 201
Website: loch-lomond.co.uk

Fine dining with a magnificent view.

Lychee Oriental Chinese Restaurant

59 Mitchell Street
Glasgow
G1 3LN
Telephone: 0141 248 2240
Website: lycheeoriental.co.uk

Traditional Chinese cooking techniques and natural, fresh ingredients create a superior dining experience featuring cuisines across Asia.

Madha Indian Restaurant

42 Albion Street
Glasgow
G1 1LH
Telephone: 0141 552 6000
Website: madha.co.uk

A family owned restaurant serving traditional Indian cuisine.

Mussel Inn

157 Hope Street
Glasgow
G2 2UQ
Telephone: 0141 572 1405
Website: mussel-inn.com

Mussel Inn is one of Scotland's most popular seafood restaurants.

Nanika

72 Victoria Road
Glasgow
G42 7AA
Telephone: 07383 716 676
Website: nanika2.neocities.org

Small eatery that's big on flavour and fun, centred around Asian cuisine with noodles and steamed buns in the spotlight.

The Oystercatcher

Otter Ferry
Tighnabruaich
PA21 2DH
Telephone: 01700 821 229
Website: theoystercatcher.co.uk

The best food from the Cowal Peninsula and Argyll.

Partick Duck Club

27 Hyndland Street
Glasgow
G11 5QF
Telephone: 0141 334 9909
Website: partickduckclub.co.uk

Stylish restaurant featuring classic favourites.

Pickled Ginger

512 St Vincent Street
Glasgow
G3 8XZ
Telephone: 0141 328 8941
Website: pickledgingerfinnieston.co.uk

A Japanese and Korean fusion restaurant set amongst the coolest spots in Glasgow.

Piece

14 Waterloo Street
Glasgow
G2 6DB
Telephone: 0141 204 3549
Website: pieceglasgow.com

Sandwich shop with a big personality.

Rioja

1116 Argyle Street
Glasgow
G3 8TD
Telephone: 0141 334 0761
Website: riojafinnieston.co.uk

Tapas restaurant and late night cocktail bar.

Sannino Pizzaria

61 Elmbank St
Glasgow
G2 4PQ
Telephone: 0141 332 3565
Website: sannino.co.uk

A little taste of Italy in the heart of the city centre.

Sloans

108 Argyle Street
Glasgow
G2 8BG
Telephone: 0141 221 8886
Website: sloansglasgow.com

Historic, vibrant venue serving up comfort food favourites.

So L.A.

43 Mitchell Street
Between Argyle St and Gordon St
Glasgow
G1 3LA
Telephone: 0141 473 7333
Website: solaglasgow.com

Inspired by the bold, exciting flavours of the Californian dining scene.

Spanish Butcher

80 Miller Street
Glasgow
G1 1DT
Telephone: 0141 406 9880
Website: spanishbutcher.com

Combines Spanish and Mediterranean inspired flavours with the finest grade meats.

Spitfire Espresso

127 Candleriggs
Merchant City
Glasgow
G1 1NP
Telephone: 0757 825 0105
Website: spitfireespresso.com

Coffee and eggs done well in a hip café.

Saint Luke's & The Winged Ox

17 Bain Street
Calton
G40 2Jz
Telephone: 0141 552 8378
Website: stlukesglasgow.com

International comfort food and quirky flavours in a music bar setting.

Sugar Boat

30 Colquhoun Square
Helensburgh
G84 8AQ
Telephone: 01436 647 522
Website: sugarboat.co.uk

Hearty bistro foods with local flavours.

Tantrum Doughnuts

27 Old Dumbarton Road
Glasgow
G3 8RD
Telephone: 0141 339 9319
Website: tantrumdoughnuts.com

Delectable brioche doughnuts, prepared with love.

Two Fat Ladies at The Buttery

652 Argyle Street
Glasgow
G3 8UF
Telephone: 0141 221 8188
Website: twofatladiesrestaurant.com

Landmark Glasgow restaurant with acclaimed seafood menu.

Ubiquitous Chip

12 Ashton Lane
Glasgow
G12 8SJ
Telephone: 0141 334 5007
Website: ubiquitouschip.co.uk

A memorable dining experience inspired by Scottish regional dishes.

Wild Fig

31 Carron Place (AKP Building)
Kelvin
East Kilbride
G75 0YL
Telephone: 0755 120 3166
Website: wildfigfood.com

Family business using simple, natural ingredients.

Other titles in the 'Get Stuck In' series

***The Manchester Cook Book:
Second Helpings***
features Ben Mounsey of
Grafene, Hatch, Refuge,
Masons, Old School BBQ Bus
and lots more.
978-1-910863-44-2

***The Cardiff & South Wales
Cook Book***
features James Sommerin of
Restaurant James Sommerin,
Cocorico Patisserie, Sosban
and lots more.
978-1-910863-31-2

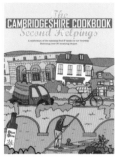

***The Cambridgeshire Cook Book:
Second Helpings***
features Mark Abbott of
Midsummer House, The Olive
Grove, Elder Street Café and
lots more.
978-1-910863-33-6

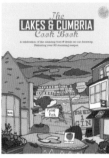

***The Lakes & Cumbria
Cook Book***
features Simon Rogan's
L'Enclume, Forest Side,
Hawkshead Relish,
L'al Churrasco and lots more.
978-1-910863-30-5

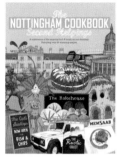

***The Nottingham Cook Book:
Second Helpings***
features Welbeck Estate,
Memsaab, Sauce Shop, 200
Degrees Coffee, Homeboys,
Rustic Crust and lots more.
978-1-910863-27-5

The Devon Cook Book
sponsored by Food Drink
Devon features Simon
Hulstone of The Elephant,
Noel Corston, Riverford Field
Kitchen and much more.
978-1-910863-24-4

The South London Cook Book
features Jose Pizarro, Adam
Byatt, The Alma, Piccalilli
Caff, Canopy Beer, Inkspot
Brewery and lots more.
978-1-910863-27-5

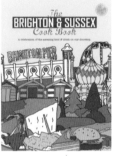

***The Brighton & Sussex Cook
Book*** features Steven Edwards,
The Bluebird Tea Co, Isaac At,
Real Patisserie, Sussex Produce
Co, and lots more.
978-1-910863-22-0

The Liverpool Cook Book
features Burnt Truffle, The
Art School, Fraîche, Villaggio
Cucina and many more.
978-1-910863-15-2

The Bristol Cook Book
features Dean Edwards, Lido,
Clifton Sausage, The Ox, and
wines from Corks of Cotham
plus lots more.
978-1-910863-14-5

The Leeds Cook Book
features The Boxtree,
Crafthouse, Stockdales of
Yorkshire and lots more.
978-1-910863-18-3

The Cotswolds Cook Book
features David Everitt-
Matthias of Champignon
Sauvage, Prithvi, Chef's Dozen
and lots more.
978-0-9928981-9-9

The Shropshire Cook Book
features Chris Burt of The
Peach Tree, Old Downton
Lodge, Shrewsbury Market,
CSons and lots more.
978-1-910863-32-9

The Norfolk Cook Book
features Richard Bainbridge,
Morston Hall, The Duck Inn
and lots more.
978-1-910863-01-5

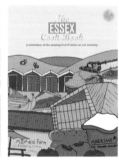

The Essex Cook Book features
Thomas Leatherbarrow,
The Anchor Riverside, Great
Garnetts, Deersbrook Farm,
Mayfield Bakery and
lots more.
978-1-910863-25-1

*All books in this series are available from Waterstones,
Amazon and independent bookshops.*

FIND OUT MORE ABOUT US AT WWW.MEZEPUBLISHING.CO.UK